Teaching Adults in the Sunday School

GAINES S. DOBBINS

CONVENTION PRESS
NASHVILLE, TENNESSEE

Printed in the United States of America
15. F 57 R.R.D.

Affectionately Dedicated to

DOCTOR JOHN RICHARD SAMPEY

Friend of God

Follower of Christ

Interpreter of the Scriptures

Teacher of Teachers

Champion of the Sunday School

ABOUT THE AUTHOR

Gaines Stanley Dobbins, a native Mississippian, received degrees from Mississippi College, the Southern Baptist Theological Seminary, and Columbia University. He served as pastor in Mississippi, then for five years was on the editorial staff of the Baptist Sunday School Board, and for thirty-six years was on the faculty of Southern Seminary, Louisville, Kentucky. In 1956 he joined the faculty of Golden Gate Baptist Theological Seminary, Berkeley, California, with the title of Distinguished Professor of Church Administration.

For four decades Dr. Dobbins has sought to lift the level of teaching and training in Southern Baptist churches. Teaching ministers and other Christian workers in a theological seminary, he has influenced generation after generation of Baptist leaders to give teaching and training a major place in their ministry. In local churches and in assemblies he has touched thousands of lay workers and imparted to them his enthusiasm for qualitative results. He has probably written more Sunday school lesson expositions, more Training Union programs, and more articles dealing with popular religious education than any other living Southern Baptist. His score of books have had national and international circulation.

Dr. Dobbins has served on numerous committees of the Southern Baptist Convention, and is co-chairman of the Commission on Bible Study and Membership Training of the Baptist World Alliance. Retiring from the deanship of Louisville, Kentucky, Dr. Dobbins, with his wife, now lives at 1451 Thousand Oaks Boulevard, Albany, California.

THE SUNDAY SCHOOL TRAINING COURSE

The Sunday School Training Course prepared by the Sunday School Department of the Baptist Sunday School Board is one of the major means of promoting Sunday school work. Its influence is limited only by its use.

The six sections of the course include studies in Bible, doctrines, evangelism, Sunday school leadership and administration, teaching, age group studies, and special studies. The range of the course is broad, for the field of Sunday school work is broad and requires comprehensive and specific training. Sixteen books are required for the completion of each Diploma.

The study of the Training Course is not to be limited to the present Sunday school workers. Most churches need twice as many workers as are now enlisted. This need can be supplied by training additional workers now. Members of the Young People's and Adult classes and older Intermedites should be led to study these books, for thereby will their service be assured. Parents will find help as they study what the Sunday school is trying to do.

SPECIAL NOTE TO INSTRUCTORS:

During your teaching of this book will you check with the Sunday school superintendent and see if an accurate record of training for the workers is kept. If not, please urge him to set up such a file with an associate superintendent of training in charge. File cards for this purpose may be ordered at nominal cost from your nearest Baptist Book Store.

A. V. WASHBURN

Secretary, Teaching and Training
Sunday School Department
Baptist Sunday School Board

CONTENTS

Adults are funny animals, but:
1. A growing % of the population
2. largest span of life
3. those who guide all of life for everyone
4. necessary to God's Church & Kingdom
5. In need of Personal Salvation & Service

CHAPTER I

OUR MISUNDERSTOOD ADULTS

OUTLINE

1. Adults Are Not Grown-up Children
2. Adults Are Not All Alike
3. Adults Are Not too Old to Learn
4. Adults Have Not Lost the Capacity for Romance
5. Adults Have Not Outgrown the Possibility of Change
6. Adults Are Not Hardened to the Claims of Christ
7. Adults Are Not too Busy to Serve

Life is like a stream. Beginning at the cradle, it winds its way inevitably to the grave as a river flows from its source to the sea. Out of eternity comes life, and into eternity it flows. Between the beginning and the end of this mortal life there are stages of growth and change that merge almost imperceptibly into each other, as the tributaries of the river increase its width and depth in its progress toward its destination.

The largest stretch of this life-stream is adulthood. It is the significant portion of life for which the previous stages were a preparation. Beginning about the twenty-fifth year, it runs its course toward completion of the ancient norm of three score years and ten. Modern medical science tends to lengthen this average for the more fortunate, though the strain of life reduces it for many. A striking fact, brought out by study of population trends in the United States, is that the proportion of elderly people is constantly increasing, while that of young people is decreasing. Study the following table, giving population of the United States for 1870 and 1930, with estimates based on figures considered reliable by the

United States Census Bureau, showing number and per
cent of total of those under 25 years of age and over 25
years of age, for 1940, 1950, and 1960:

	Under 25 Years of Age		25 Years of Age and Over	
Year	Number	Per Cent	Number	Per Cent
1870	22,904,502	59.4	15,653,869	40.6
1930	58,479,369	47.6	64,295,677	52.4
1940	57,053,800	43.3	74,811.400	56.7
1950	53,099,100	38.4	85,342,600	61.6
1960	49,787,500	35.2	91,697,000	64.8

The startling revelation is made by these statistics and
estimates that in the sixty years between 1870 and 1930
the number of children and young people in the United
States has *decreased* nearly 12 per cent, while the number of adults has *increased* in exactly the same ratio. The
estimates are still more startling, indicating as they do
that by 1940 there will probably be 13.4 per cent more
adults than children and young people; by 1950, a 23.2
per cent increase of adults; and by 1960, a 29.6 increase of adults over children and young people. Of
course these estimates are forecasts based on present
trends, and many things may happen to change these
trends before 1960, but the fact stands out undeniably
that we have a vast and growing population of adults
and a decreasing population of children and young people.

Thus we see that, from the standpoint both of numbers and of life span, adults constitute increasingly the
most important group in our American life.

Yet it is safe to say that, educationally and religiously,
they are the most neglected and misunderstood group.
This book proposes a fresh study of adults, their capacities and needs, their possibilities and difficulties, their
interests and abilities; and how the modern Bible class
and Adult department of the Sunday school may be made
one of the most valuable of agencies for the Christian
education and utilization of adults.

We must begin with the effort better to understand these often misunderstood adults. Let us seek first of all to clear up certain pretty general misconceptions.

1. *Adults Are Not Grown-up Children*

[handwritten marginalia: 1. Minds & Emotions have grown with bodies 2. Need childlike attributes, but not childishness. 3. Are capable of & appreciate serious thought 4. Won't respond unless challenged]

Paul, in his immortal ode to love, declares that when he was a child he thought, spoke and acted as a child; but when he became a man he put away childish things. Nevertheless, Jesus states with great positiveness that except one turn and become as a child he cannot enter the kingdom of heaven. The ideal thus discovered is that of maturity characterized by the fine qualities of childhood. There are some attributes of the child which are essential to the man—faith, reverence, guilelessness, affection, sincerity, teachableness. But it is a pity when a man, instead of being *childlike*, becomes *childish*— credulous, emotionally unstable, dependent, impulsive, short-sighted, shallow-minded, self-centered. Not all men and women who have achieved the years of maturity have become grown-up mentally and spiritually. Such people are poorly adjusted to life, and make living difficult both for themselves and for others.

It is a mistake for an adult to be thought of as a grown-up child. This mistake is made when a Sunday school class is organized and conducted as if its members were children, incapable of serious thought and independent action. To be sure, some adults seem to like to be babied, but a prime purpose of adult religious education is to change this unfortunate attitude and develop men and women who can think and act for themselves and who have learned the joy of being creative and self-directing. Let us agree that the purposes of God in Christ can never be accomplished by adults who have the notion that they are just children grown to years of accountability.

2. *Adults Are Not All Alike*   *[handwritten marginalia: Many sizes, shapes, forms]*

Women say, "Oh, all men are alike." Men say, "Well, you know all women are alike." Of course neither are right. True, there are traits possessed by adult men and women in common, since they are human beings and pass through many of the same experiences; but their differences are even greater than their similarities.

One of the most fascinating of studies is that of varieties of human beings. All sorts of classifications have been attempted, none of which are entirely satisfactory. Look at this classification and try to put yourself and members of your Sunday school class in the list that seems best to describe you and them:

(1) Happy, well-adjusted, successful Christians, who have found the will of God for their lives, and are living examples of the blessedness that Christ promises to those who abide in him, and in whom his word abides.

(2) Christians who live on the borderline—compromising between the ideal of the Spirit and the call of the world; sometimes warm and sometimes cold in the their Christian devotion; half-hearted and undependable in their service; too religious to be happy out in the world, and too worldly to be happy in Christ.

(3) Backslidden, cold, indifferent Christians, defeated and overborne in their spirits; men and women who have lost out, at least for the time, in the struggle against temptation; to whom Christ, the church, the Bible, prayer, and Christian fellowship have largely faded from consciousness as possessing reality and power.

(4) The sick, the heart-broken, the poverty-stricken, the down-and-out, who have lost step in the onward march of affairs, and whom the world is passing by with little apparent notice or concern; men and women who have wearily concluded that nothing much matters, and who doubt the love of Christ and the providence of God for them.

(5) Aggressive, self-confident men and women, who like to take the lead and who welcome responsibility; some of whom are using their abilities for Christ, while others are putting self first.

6. Backward

(6) Timid, hesitant men and women, who shrink from notice and responsibility, some because of lack of native ability, some because they are underprivileged, others because of bashful disposition.

7. Spiritually dead

(7) The spiritually ignorant men and women who know next to nothing about the Bible and the things of religion, and who are accordingly indifferent to spiritual interests, or who have an inward feeling of inferiority in the presence of those who possess such advantages.

8. Odd-balls

(8) Men and women with twisted personality—the "queer," "cranky," "peculiar" people who are hard to get along with, and who often are easily offended and estranged.

9. mental cases

(9) The mentally defective—unfortunate people who have not developed intelligence beyond that of a child, from whom mature judgment and conduct cannot be expected.

10. Unregenerate

(10) Moral and spiritual rebels—those who have rejected the claims of Christ and the standards of the New Testament, and who are living in sin and unbelief —some because of long spiritual neglect and delay, others because of deliberate determination to put self ahead of the will of God.

3. *Adults Are Not too Old to Learn*

Man has the capacity to learn + discern

Looking at the vast number of adults about us who are poorly adjusted, inadequately equipped, unhappy and defeated, lost and undone, are not our hearts filled with a great compassion for them? What can be done about it? Some are ready to say sadly, "Nothing; they are too old to learn." Let us analyze this age-old fallacy.

from with it — does not lose it until extreme old age

"You can't teach an old dog new tricks," says some one with an air of finality. There are two things the matter with this adage. First, people are not dogs; second, it is not proposed to teach them tricks. One of the marks that forever distinguishes the human being from the highest animal order is man's capacity to learn.

Children — better "permanent memory"
Adults — " "Immediate " "

This capacity he inherits from birth, and, barring defectiveness, illness, or accident, this original power of mind in man continues undiminished until the onset of physical decline in old age.

Many experiments have been conducted in recent years that demonstrate the continued ability of adults to learn. It is true that what is learned in childhood is retained longer. The "permanent memory" of the child is superior to that of the adults; but the "immediate memory" of the adult is ordinarily much superior to that of the child. You may try this out for yourself. Put a group of children and a group of adults at work committing certain facts to memory. Invariably the adults will score higher in their ability to reproduce immediately, though the children will remember longer what they have learned.

Learning, however, consists of much more than the power to memorize. To learn is to discover how to meet new and novel situations, to profit by experience, to develop better ways of thinking and behaving. The adult is far better equipped for this kind of learning than the child. He has greater powers of logical reasoning, a richer background of experience, and better techniques for carrying on the learning processes. Thus considered, is it not much more reasonable to expect adults to surpass children in the ability to learn?

Back of the old saying that "adults are too old to learn" is a half-truth. Many adults, as they grow older, cease to learn. They close their minds to new ideas, they give up to mental laziness, and their powers of learning atrophy, just as a muscle that is not used. Learning is not automatic, but requires effort. There is such a thing as "sweat of brain" as well as of body, and the adult who quits trying to learn soon finds himself mentally stagnant. One of the greatest services which a Sunday school class can perform is that of keeping adults "awake in the head"—learners, with alert, inquiring minds all their lives.

Adults cease to learn — not because they can't — but because they won't! We need to keep adults learning.

4. *Adults Have Not Lost the Capacity for Romance*

Youth, we are told, is the time of romance and adventure. Maturity, we are informed, is the period of stern reality. Occasionally some man or woman, past middle life, attempts the romantic, whereupon we are reminded that there is "no fool like an old fool." Is it true that life loses its romantic quality and its adventurous zest as we leave the realm of adolescence with its love-making and its daring?

There is a story of a visitor who was being entertained in a home where he had not yet met his hostess. Next morning at breakfast a silver-haired lady of some seventy years greeted him at the breakfast table. "Mrs. Smith, I presume?" said he. "No," she smiled, "I am Miss Jones, Mrs. Smith's sister." "Oh," said he, as he took her hand, "so you are not married." "No," she shyly replied, "not yet."

Yes, hope springs eternal. And so does the romance of life, and so does the love of adventure. Watch the crowds that throng a glamorously romantic picture show, or a thrillingly exciting sporting event. Observe the large proportion of those who are adults, and the number who are elderly matrons and men past middle life. The truth is that multitudes of grown-ups are starved for romance and adventure and turn to the maudlin and artificial to supply that which their natures crave but which they are denied from wholesome, natural sources.

For romance is more than love-making and adventure than youthful daring. It would not be natural for the romance of youth to be the romance of adulthood, and the adventure which stirs the blood of twenty becomes absurd at forty. But it is tragedy when the spirit of true romance and high adventure dies in any human heart. Think of the romance of home-making, of the rearing of children, of establishing new ties of friendship, of blessing other lives, of living for Christ and his kingdom! Think of the adventure of new enterprises, of worthy achievement, of fresh discoveries, of courageously

standing for the right, of winning others to Christ and
his cause, of joining in the greatest of all crusades—the
bringing in of the kingdom of God! When men and
women lose the capacity to thrill to the call of such romance and adventure as this, they are indeed to be pitied.

It takes religion to keep life fresh and zestful. For
Christianity the Golden Age is not in the past but in
the future. Life is never dull for the active Christian,
for the unexpected is always happening. When the
church and Sunday school become dull and prosaic they
are untrue to the spirit of Jesus, every moment of whose
life was crowded with the unusual. We make an inexcusable mistake when we reduce the program and teaching of adults to the stereotyped and commonplace, and
take away the challenge of the heroic. Of course there
are numberless men and women whose lives have become
dull and drab, but they need to be awakened to the romance of Christian living and to the adventure of Christian service. Does not the revival of religion for which
we long in our day await this rediscovery of the capacity
of adults for the romance of Christ's redemptive love for
all men, and for the high adventure of making the whole
world Christian?

5. *Adults Have Not Outgrown the Possibility of Change*

There is a poem which tells of plastic clay that could
be fashioned at will into any form desired, but laid
aside, grew hard and unchangeable. So, the poem tells
us, the plastic clay of childhood "hardens into man."
Another familiar analogy is that of concrete which can
be made to take any form desired while it is fresh, but
after it becomes "set" is adamant. Again the figure of
the tree is used—the tender plant may be easily trans-
planted and shaped, but the mature tree is incapable of
such change. The argument is that childhood and youth
are the only periods in which human life can be molded,
for when maturity is attained it is too late for men and
women to change.

The trouble about all such analogies, and the conclusions based on them, is that they undertake to compare disparates—things that are quite unlike. Concrete can be compared with stone, but not with human life. Clay can be compared with wax, but not with the human mind. Trees can be compared with shrubs, but not with human personality. Because a truth applies to concrete, or clay, or trees is no reason why it should apply to human beings. Many of our wrong notions grow out of this kind of false reasoning.

Human nature is *essentially* modifiable. Not much can be done to change the nature of inorganic matter, of vegetation, or of animal life. New combinations can be made, new uses discovered, improvements developed, but the essential nature of rocks and soil and birds and beasts remains much the same. Not so with human beings. The moment a baby comes into the world he begins a long and continuous process of change. Every day sees some change take place in his ideas, his attitudes, his habits. Not only does he himself change, but he constantly changes his environment. It is literally true that a normal human being is by his very nature a *changing* creature, and this process of change begins at birth and continues to death, when the greatest of all changes takes place.

Unquestionably change occurs more rapidly in the early years of life, because in these years the child is becoming adjusted to his surroundings. That which is learned in childhood is retained better, partly because it is used more frequently and over a longer period of time. Gradually the individual becomes accustomed to certain ways of thinking and acting, and if these prove measurably satisfactory no new ways are found necessary. But if novel and difficult situations arise, calling for new ways of thinking and acting to meet them, the adult can change almost as readily as the child in order to meet the emergency. The majority of adults have fallen into routine patterns of thought and conduct that take care of life's

Problems : 1. Stubbornness
2. Routine without reason
3. Fear of new

ordinary demands. Why should they change? To ex-
change the old for the new costs energy, and sometimes
is disturbing and painful. Why pay the price unless
necessary?

Life was never intended to be stagnant. We live at
our best when we meet the changing conditions about
us with changed hearts, changed minds, changed methods,
changed conduct. The very word "conversion" implies
a fundamental change at the very core of one's being,
and "repentance" in the New Testament refers to a
mind-change that takes place not once but many times
as new and higher choices replace the old lower levels.
The Christian ideal is that of growth in grace and knowledge, and growth, of necessity, involves change. One of
the high functions of a Sunday school class is the stimulation and guidance of growth—change—toward the
measure of the stature of Jesus Christ.

6. *Adults Are Not Hardened to the Claims of Christ*

There is a widely current heresy abroad that adults
can rarely if ever be won to Christ, and that the conversion of an adult is to be looked on with suspicion even
when it occurs. We are pointed to statistics that show
85 per cent of evangelical church members as coming
through the Sunday school, and under the age of sixteen.
Our attention is called to the far greater ease with which
children are led to Christ, and the economy of concen-
trating our energies on the group that yields so much
greater results in proportion to effort in winning them.
We have grown accustomed to the matter-of-fact expec-
tation that children shall come through the Cradle Roll,
Nursery, Beginner, and Primary departments, and during
the Junior and Intermediate years make a profession of
faith; while we express astonishment if adults present
themselves for baptism.

God forbid that we should depreciate the winning of
children. To such, Jesus declared, belongs his kingdom.
Nor would we for a moment deny the greater fruitfulness
of a life won early to the service of the Saviour. Yet the

Aul closer to eternity 2. need more forginues
3. Committed with larger responsibilities.
IN THE SUNDAY SCHOOL   11
4. more able to understand the gospel

fact remains that there are some forty million adults in the population of the United States who make no claim to being Christians. Is it conceivable that we shall thus lightly give them up, on the ground that they are more difficult to win than children, and do not make as useful Christians?

To what extent is the conversion of adults an all but hopeless undertaking? We have the record of a number of people who were won by Jesus himself. Every one of them was an adult! He welcomed little children, and put his arms about them in blessing, but he left the actual work of bringing them to him to others. Paul, the master soul-winner after Christ, devoted his chief energies to the winning of grown men and women. The great evangelists of history have followed in the footsteps of Jesus and Paul, and have gone forth to seek and to win the lost of every age, never despairing of the oldest and most hardened of sinners.

Do we not often take it too quickly for granted that adults are hopelessly hardened to the claims of Christ? Often, like Lydia, their hearts are open to the truth, and they need but be told the story of redeeming love to accept the Saviour joyously. Again, like the hard-hearted Philippian jailor, they are ready to cry in their extremity, "What must we do to be saved?" and are waiting longingly for some one to say, "Believe on the Lord Jesus Christ." To whom can the claims of Christ come with such force as to intelligent, mature men and women? Who can need more his forgiveness, his comfort, his guidance, than these same hard-pressed, sin-beset adults? We discredit our faith and cast doubt on Christ's saving mission when we cease to be deeply concerned for the multitudes of lost men and women in our midst, and to bear witness confidently to Christ's power to save unto the uttermost all who come to God through him. Sunday school teachers and officers who have lost this note of faith and compassion have surrendered their charter as true Christian workers.

7. *Adults Are Not too Busy to Serve*

"No need to call on Mr. Blank for anything—he's too busy." "Mrs. Blank is capable, but she's too busy to serve." Who are Mr. and Mrs. Blank? Their name is legion. Often they represent the most attractive personality and the highest type of ability in the church and community, but they are not enlisted to teach or to serve as officers and workers in the Sunday school because the word has gone out that they are "too busy."

Too busy doing what? Making money? Attending to secular affairs? Climbing the social ladder? Playing politics? Having a good time? It would be interesting to put down the names of a dozen of these pre-occupied people, and then accurately indicate how they spend their time. No doubt it would be discovered that their days are very full, but full of what? Are they happy in the realization that they are giving only the fag ends of their lives to Christian service? Perhaps it is not altogether their fault. Like the men in the parable when asked why they were not at work, they can truthfully reply, "No man hath hired us."

We have all too often assumed that busy, harassed men and women, with the burdens of business and housekeeping on them, have no time left to serve Christ. As a matter of fact, the chief reason why they are distracted and heavy-laden is because they, like Martha of old, are "cumbered with much serving" which puts the emphasis in the wrong place. Let the average over-worked adult get Christ's viewpoint, and put first things first, and the yoke will actually become easy and the burden light. There is plenty of time for Christian usefulness for the man or woman who has learned Paul's secret, "I can do all things through Christ who strengtheneth me." It is a matter of common observation that when an important task is to be performed it is always best to call on a busy person.

There are many needs in our church life today, but near the head of the list stands the need for competent, consecrated Christian service. Why does the program of many a church lag? Why is the Sunday school poorly administered? Why is there chronic undersupply of workers in the Training Union? Why does the progress of the Kingdom falter and halt? The one most inclusive answer, coming from pastors throughout the land, is the lack of willing and capable workers. Where are these workers to be found? For the most part in the adult Bible classes. The strategy of church and kingdom building is to enlist these capable, busy men and women in a well-organized Sunday school class, and then win them to Christ if they are unsaved, and to definite Christian service if they are church members. It is a tragic mistake to assume that they cannot be enlisted in fruitful, happy work for Christ because they are "too busy." Our Master said, "My Father worketh hitherto, and I work." He has a place of usefulness in his vast redemptive program for every man and woman who will hear and heed his call. A Sunday school class is at its best when it is translating the teachings of the Book into deeds of loving helpfulness in imitation of him who "went about doing good."

We are now ready to ask ourselves as teachers, Do we understand these men and women whom we teach? Have we assumed a good deal about them as true which has no basis in fact? Do we fully realize the importance of understanding these adults in order to teach them successfully? It was said of Jesus, the Master Teacher, that he knew what was in man. Let us study and pray unceasingly that we may attain, in our measure, to something of this insight which is at the heart of all successful teaching!

AIDS TO LEARNING

1. List at least a half-dozen assumptions commonly made concerning adults that are only partially true.
2. Make a list of a dozen members of your class, as unlike as possible. On the basis of the tenfold classification given on pages 4 and 5, indicate which description best fits each person. To what conclusion does this lead?

3. Suppose, in soliciting a number of adults to join your Sunday school, they should decline on the ground that they are "too old to learn." How would you answer them?

4. How may a Sunday school class meet the need of adults for romance and adventure?

5. Why is it easier to win children than adults to Christ? How old do you think an unsaved person should be before we give him up? Why are not more adults won?

6. Of what value would it be to the teacher to be a diligent student of adult life, using his or her class as a laboratory?

ch. 2 —→

Remember — we teach,
not lessons, but people.
What is the dif between Organization
+ Organism? —
must not seek goals for the group
but growth for the individuals

1, An Adult must know himself
2, " " " " others
3, A teacher of Adults must know both well

CHAPTER II

GETTING READY FOR ADULTHOOD

OUTLINE

Adults have stages of growth!

1. Growth a Continuous Process
2. Childhood, the Foundation-Laying Years
3. Adolescence, the Period of Adjustment
4. The Importance of a Good Beginning

The ancient philosopher said, "Know thyself!" The modern psychologist says, "Behave yourself!" The man of the streets says, "Act your age!" The poet says: "Self-reverence, self-knowledge, and self-control—these three alone lead life to sovereign power." The philosopher, the physchologist, the practical man of affairs, and the poet agree on the necessity of knowing oneself and understanding others if life is to be lived at its best. Workers with adults must understand adults. That means, first of all, that they must understand themselves. There is a vast difference between teaching *lessons* and teaching *people*. It makes all the difference in the world if we think in terms of an *organization* rather than in terms of an *organism*. A Sunday school class, if it functions worthily, is a living thing, made up of living men or women, each one of whom must be studied, nurtured, exercised, to the end that there may be continuous growth. There are stages of growth in adulthood just as there are in childhood and youth. We turn now to a study of these several levels of development in the lives of growing men and women.

1. *Growth a Continuous Process*

Somewhere between the ages of sixteen and twenty the average individual "gets his growth." That is to say, the

physical body growth reaches end at 16-20 not so with mind — reach max. of native intelligence at 16 but study & practice can then continue growth

skeletal framework reaches its maximum, the vital organs and glands cease further growth, and the nervous system matures. In many respects the individual's character may be said to be formed. At birth the average male weighs 7.8, the female 7 pounds; at sixteen the average weight for the boy is 114, for the girl 110.5 pounds; at eighteen the weight has increased to 124.4 and 114.5, respectively. At twenty the young man weighs 135, the young woman remains at 114. At birth the boy baby is, on the average, 20.5 inches, the girl baby 20.3 inches tall; at sixteen height has increased to 64 inches for the boy and 63.2 for the girl; at eighteen to 67.6 and 64 inches respectively, after which further growth practically ceases. What a merciful providence of nature it is that physical growth begins to halt at about the age of sixteen and, except for a bit of broadening and filling in, comes to a standstill at about the age of twenty! Occasionally we find an individual for whom growth in weight, at least, keeps on at an alarming pace, but such a person is an exception to the general rule. Most of us count ourselves fortunate to have "got our growth" by the time we reach the close of the period of middle adolescence.

Do we get our growth socially, mentally, and spiritually in corresponding years? Accurate tests indicate that native intelligence reaches its maximum around the sixteenth year. At first it was concluded that the individual becomes mentally grown-up at about the same age that physical maturity is reached. But further study has shown this conclusion to be unsound. A field of ten acres cannot be stretched to twenty acres, but the right sort of cultivation can make a field of ten acres yield vastly more. An individual may inherit a very ordinary intellectual equipment, but this equipment can be so guided and utilized as to bring infinitely rich returns.

The most hopeful thing about human life is this power of continuous growth. The limits of the human mind have never yet been discovered. You, for instance, might have been a lawyer, a doctor, a musician, an artist, a poet, a sculptor, a teacher, an architect, an engineer, a farmer, a mechanic, a business man or woman, and so on down the long line of vocations to which men and women, find themselves called. Why is there little hope of your achieving mastery in more than one or two of these lines? Why, mainly, for the lack of time! Before we realize it we are fifty years old, and the remaining twenty or thirty years scarcely suffice for the use of the little we have acquired of knowledge and skill.

Eternity is demanded for the unfolding of man's mental and spiritual powers. Is it not inconceivable that a wise God would have involved such possibilities as are latent in every man and woman and then make no provision for these possibilities to be realized? Thank God, life in Christ is eternal! Growth in mind, character, personality, soul—call it what you will—is continuous. Life's greatest single purpose is to provide the best possible conditions for this growth, from stage to stage of human development, always with a view to the life beyond this life, for which the present life is but a preparation.

2. *Childhood, the Foundation-Laying Years*

By the time one reaches maturity life has grown exceedingly complex. Myriad streams of influence have poured in, each stimulus bringing some corresponding response, and each response exerting some power in the formation of the total personality. How can we *know* the resultant individual? Have you not often been puzzled over people whose ideas and behaviour you could not understand? "How," you have asked yourselves, "did they get that way?" And quite likely others have asked the same question about you! How get the key to an understanding of men and women thirty, forty, fifty, sixty years of age?

The modern science of human nature, psychology, tells us where to start. To understand the man we must go back to the child. A noted student of human develop-

1st yr. perhaps most important.
Certainly 1-3 — Problems often are traced back to childhood

ment declares that the first year is the greatest year in any person's life. Another eminent authority declares that more is done for the ultimate character of the individual in the first three years than in all the remaining years of life. When life breaks down so that the expert in the field of personality and mental disorders must be called in, he at once begins to trace the difficulty to its hidden childhood origins. It is now being discovered that most of the "peculiarities" that mar human character are the result of unfortunate childhood experiences that set up tendencies that have never been outgrown. In many cases these difficulties might be overcome if they were understood. At any rate, there would come a new appreciation of the individual struggling with the handicap of warps and twists in his personality if we realized more fully that these defects were not so much due to "pure meanness" as to circumstances over which, in the beginning at least, he had little control.

Two influences combine to shape the early life of the child. One of these powerful forces is heredity. The law of heredity is that like tends to beget like. The child receives one-half of his inherited traits from his immediate parents, one-fourth from his grandparents, one-eighth from his great-grandparents, one-sixteenth from his great, great-grandparents, and so on until the vanishing point is reached. This general rule has several important variations. There is, for instance, the fact of "dominance" and "recessiveness." From the "dominant" parent may come nearly all of a child's inherited traits, while the traits from the "recessive" parent do not appear until the next generation. This accounts, in part, for the tendency of certain characteristics to skip a generation. Then, too, certain characteristics appear to be handed down as units, and a given unit of inheritance may suddenly reappear after being absent for several generations. This explains the red-haired child whose parents and grandparents and even great-grandparents were all black haired. Think of the many streams of inheritance that have come together in the making of a new individual. The complexity of these combinations is almost overwhelming. In order to understand a given individual, therefore, it is necessary to know as much as possible about his family line. It is not always practicable to secure this information, but frequently the thoughtful teacher or class officer can go back to the inheritance of an individual who is hard to understand and get an entirely new slant on his peculiarities and difficulties.

Fully as important as heredity in the shaping of personality is the power of _environment._ Indeed, we are thinking much today in terms of "social heredity" as a better word than "environment." Just as the individual inherits color, facial features, size, and similar physical characteristics, so he just as truly inherits language, customs, standards, ideals, and the vast accumulation of possessions that we call "social." From the moment of birth these environmental influences affect the child, shaping his knowledge, his attitudes, his choices, his conduct. It follows, therefore, that before the child has reached the age where he can make logical decisions, his personality has been greatly influenced by what he has learned from others, by habits that have been developed through imitation, and by standards that he has unconsciously accepted. When a given individual is under consideration, whose ways of thinking and acting cannot be easily understood, it is clarifying to ask: What were his early childhood influences? In what sort of surroundings did he grow up? How and by whom was his thinking first directed? Whose example did he follow as a child? In what kind of home was he reared? In what sort of neighborhood did he live? Where and how long did he go to school? Were there any unfortunate experiences in his early childhood that are reflected now? Again, it is not easy to arrive accurately at answers to these questions. Even so, the very asking of them often throws new light on a man or woman who must be understood if reached for Christ, won to a life of Christian service, and aided to overcome the hindrances that stand in the way of strong, well-rounded Christian character.

3. Adolescence, the Period of Adjustment

By "adolescence" is meant that period of life which
lies between childhood and maturity. In terms of years
it represents the ages between twelve and twenty-four.
It is the second dozen of years of the normal life span.
During these years the transition is made from the dependence of childhood to the independence of maturity;
from the powers and abilities of the child to those of the
man or woman; from the social and spiritual relationships
of childhood to the moral responsibilities of adulthood.
During the first dozen years the foundations of character are being laid; during the next dozen years the
superstructure is being built. It is impossible to over-
estimate the importance of these transition years of
adolescence.

dependence to independence

First, *physical adjustments of far-reaching importance
take place.* There is rapid increase in weight and a corresponding spurt of growth in height. Heart and lungs
attain their maximum growth, glands of internal secre-
tion, particularly the sex glands, develop their full powers
and functions; the nervous system, including the brain,
attains maturity. The demands of the growing body put
a heavy strain on physical resources, and this overstrain
is liable to bring about many unhappy results. On the
one hand, physical and nervous breakdowns may occur;
on the other, there may be rebellion and delinquency.
Happy the man or woman whose parents and teachers
understood and appreciated these facts during this period
of physical stress and strain!

time of stress & strain

Second, *significant mental changes occur.* There is a
general deepening of the mental life, as the logical facul-
ties develop and experiences broaden. A new intellectual
world is entered with promotion to high school, and this
new world broadens into a new universe for those who
go on to college. The curiosity of the child often deepens
into skepticism, and questions arise as to the very existence of God, the authority of the Bible, the reality
of the claims of Christ, the value of the church, the

logic reason

lay aside childish faith - perhaps become skeptical

need religious adjustment - or will lose faith or be gullible to false teachers - "isms"

worthwhileness of the Christian life. For some these questions find satisfactory answer through the guidance of wise, sympathetic parents and teachers, and they move happily out into well-adjusted Christian living. For all too many others, their questioning is suppressed, or they reach no satisfactory conclusions, and thus they are sent out into life with inadequate or false views, crippled in their thinking concerning life's most momentous subjects.

It is tragic to observe how many adults have never learned to think straight concerning great moral and spiritual issues. Let any long-haired crank come to a community, begin to preach and teach some new "ism," and no matter how absurd it may be, he will soon gather about him a group of gullible adults. People thus misled are not just the ignorant and mentally defective. Often they belong to the upper circles of the thoughtful and able men and women of the community. The best explanation is that, during the period when they were adjusting their thinking in other realms, they failed to make a satisfactory religious adjustment. Consequently they never acquired tools of accurate religious thought, nor the content of a valid religious faith. Yet their hungry religious nature urges them on restlessly to discover something that will meet their inner needs. Some persuasive quack comes along with a substitute for real religion and they "fall for it." Are there not scores of adults thus misled in every community?

Often common sense will prevent men and women from being duped by false religious teachers. To them, however, the whole subject may become confused, and they pass it by as a mystery. You would not have to go far in any community to find more or less intelligent men and women who have seemingly lost all interest in religion. When they were adjusting life to its fundamental needs, during the critical years of adolescence, they failed to get the necessary help and left religion on the outside of the circle. The starved spiritual nature of such people still craves satisfaction, and this they try to find in all sorts of futile ways. Perhaps a man absorbs him-self in his work, or his lodge, or in some pet hobby, and calls that his religion. Perhaps a woman enslaves herself to her children, or to her household duties, or to club work, or to some charitable organization, in the vain hope that it will satisfy her unmet religious craving. Some-times they join the church and attend in a half-hearted sort of way, hoping against hope that the peace their souls crave will somehow come. We cannot understand these religious misfits until we realize something of the poverty of their spiritual backgrounds as children, and their failure to make a satisfactory adjustment in their religious thinking in adolescence.

Third, *there are far-reaching social adjustments* that take place during the adolescent years. During the earlier years of this period boys and girls grow intensely self-conscious. They often become restless, secretive, adven-turous. Sometimes they rebel against the discipline of home and school, often leaving school and occasionally running away from home. More young people start on a career of delinquency and crime at about sixteen than at any other age. At the same time, this is the age when they make decisions for great careers, and start on lives of highest usefulness. The years that follow are the love-making, romantic, mating years of life. By twenty-four most young people are married, and have begun the serious business of home-making and earning a liveli-hood.

Not all these young people become socially well-ad-justed. Some miss the mark so far as to become crimi-nals. Others get warped in their social nature, and grow to be undesirable members of society. As neighbors they are hard to get along with, as mothers and fathers they are selfish and critical, as church members they are cold and unloving. Has not your community its full quota of these socially maladjusted adults? We can understand them better and help them more when we understand the relation between cause and effect, the primary cause being failure to make happy social adjustment during the formative years of adolescence.

Fourth, *there are spiritual adjustments in adolescence* of utmost consequence. To the child, right is that which is approved and commanded; wrong is that which is disapproved and forbidden. The adolescent begins to make independent moral judgments, and to seek for a sounder basis of discrimination between right and wrong. Often the boy or girl becomes greatly confused. What once seemed to be right now appears to be wrong; and wrong looks as if it sometimes might be right. The highest standards of the New Testament are taught and believed on Sunday, but another standard seems to be in effect on Monday. Some teach one thing about religion, others teach something else. Disillusionment comes as the lives of professing Christians are discovered to be inconsistent. What is taught in Sunday school is often contradicted by what is taught in high school. Is it any wonder that the youth grows perplexed, discouraged, troubled?

Where guidance has been wise and the youth has been surrounded by genuine Christians who are living a vital, positive Christian life, the spiritual adjustment is usually made happily and successfully. But for many this adjustment is never made, and for a tragically large number it is made so unsatisfactorily that they never become victorious, fruitful Christians. There is a great multitude of men and women in every community who have never had a saving experience of grace. They are *lost* in all that this terrible word means. Others have made an initial acceptance of Christ, but they have never found for themselves a place of happy usefulness in his service. Look about you and observe the scores and hundreds of unenlisted, inactive adult church members. Don't be too hard on them. In many cases they have been more sinned against than sinning. At a time when they were making life's great adjustments, during the plastic years of adolescence, they were no doubt overlooked and neglected. The task of bringing them to spiritual vitality is more difficult now, but it is far from hopeless. Is not this the supreme business of the adult Sunday school class?

4. *The Importance of a Good Beginning*

As we contemplate these years of preparation for adulthood, are we not impressed afresh with the importance of a good beginning? Looking back over the first twenty-four years of any life, it is not difficult to recognize that many mistakes were made. Recognizing the point at which the mistakes occurred, it is the part of common sense to face the facts and make whatever correction is still possible. Often just to get unfortunate childhood or youthful experiences out in the open, and examine them frankly in the light of adult wisdom, is to gain a new understanding of oneself. Likewise, to go back to the childhood and youth of the men and women with whom you must deal in your work as a Sunday school teacher or officer is to get a new viewpoint of appreciation of their personality problems and peculiarities. Viewing men and women thus objectively and intelligently, you are in far better position to interest them, to meet their needs, and to enlist them in the work of the class, the department and the church.

Realization of the importance of a good beginning carries with it another distinct value. As adults our highest responsibility is that of rearing children of our own. Ought it not to be possible to avoid some of the mistakes that were made in our upbringing and to guide our children into richer and fuller Christian living? There are many forms of failure, but perhaps the bitterest of all failures is that of losing our children and watching them make shipwreck of their lives. What sort of men and women do we want our children to be? When we shall have done our best, they may disappoint us; but if we do not understand them and have no definite objectives for them, we may almost certainly expect disappointment—unless some one does for them what we, their parents, should have done.

Mistakes made by Y.P. & Parents in 1st 24 yrs are very important. Knowledge of this helps in 2 ways?
1. Being Patient & Understanding with Adults

Adults must live vicariously. They have no right to live for themselves, but must put the welfare of the on-coming generation ahead of all their desires and ambitions. An adult class should be ready to give up any member at any time to become an officer or teacher in one of the younger departments. What blind, inexcusable selfishness it is for a class of adults to live for themselves, caring nothing for the children and young people who look to them for help! Is yours a self-centered, self-sufficient class? Does it object to giving up its members for service in other departments? If so, it is failing of its mission, and cheating the boys and girls, who are to be the adults of a few years hence, of their right of a good beginning.

We cannot teach people whom we do not know; and we cannot understand the men and women whom we would teach unless we are acquainted with something of their personal history. Are you, as a teacher of adults, willing to take the time and trouble to learn what you can about their family connections, their childhood and adolescent experiences, and the formative influences which have made them what they are? If so, you are in fellowship with the Great Teacher, who said: "I am the good shepherd; and I know mine own, and mine own know me."

AIDS TO LEARNING

1. Think of several people who are difficult to understand. What would you need to know about their parentage in order to understand them better? What should you know about their childhood experiences?

2. Why is adolescence naturally a period of doubt and difficulty? What are the consequences if mental adjustment in religious matters is made poorly during these years?

3. What makes life socially difficult and dangerous between seventeen and twenty-four?

4. Why is the period of youth of such great importance spiritually? What are some of the most noticeable consequences in adult life when unsatisfactory religious adjustments are made in youth?

5. Thinking back over your childhood and youth, point out at least three grave mistakes that were made that you would like to see your children, or children whom you influence, avoid.

6. What use do you think a teacher of adults can profitably make of knowledge gathered concerning the early history of those whom he or she teaches?

CHAPTER III

STAGES IN ADULT GROWTH

OUTLINE

1. Early Maturity, the Period of Burden Bearing
2. Middle Life, the Period of Burden Bearing
3. Old Age, Life's Testing Time
4. The Importance of Individual Differences
5. Our Changed and Changing Adult World
6. Making the Most of Adulthood

We have long recognized stages in the growth of children and young people. We separate the Nursery babies from the Beginners, confining the former group to children three years of age and under, and the latter to children four and five years of age. We then put the Primaries, six to eight years of age, in a separate department, with separate classes for each age. Juniors, nine to twelve, are recognized as being a distinct group and are placed in a department of their own. Intermediates, thirteen to sixteen, likewise constitute a separate department, as do the young people, seventeen to twenty-four. Long experience has approved these age divisions.

When we come to the adults, however, we have commonly thought of them as making up a single age group. There has been rather general agreement that men and women should be in separate classes, but we have taken it for granted that a successful class could be made up of men or women of all ages above the young people's limit. On this mistaken basis, the effort has often been made to have one large class of men and one large class of women—the bigger the better. Study and experience have demonstrated the necessity of age-divisions in the adult department, and that there is almost as little justification for one large class of adult men or women as there would be for one large class made up of all the children or of all the Intermediates and young people. There are perhaps as wide differences between the interests and needs, and therefore in the character of teaching, of an adult of thirty and one of sixty as between a child of ten and a man of twenty. Let us consider the several natural levels of adult development.

1. *Early Maturity, the Period of Achievement*

The first two dozen years of life prepare the way for the succeeding four dozen. There have been a few youthful prodigies who have made their mark before twenty-five, but they are rare exceptions.

The records reveal that the great achievements of history have been made by men and women between the ages of twenty-five and fifty. Sometimes these achievements have not come to fruitage until the worker was past fifty, but rarely have men begun a new undertaking and carried it to successful fruition after the passing of the half-century mark. This period of early maturity, when life's powers are at their best, ought to be made to count tremendously for Christ and his kingdom. It is saddening to realize, however, that many men and women fritter away these precious years, and arrive at middle age with little or nothing to show for the expenditure of their time and energy.

This period of early maturity, that is from about twenty-five to forty, is for most men and women the busiest time of their lives. They are setting up their homes, the children arrive, the pressure of the daily grind at home and at work is continuous and heavy. There is for the majority a taxing financial strain. Disappointment and disillusionment are almost inevitable, as romantic dreams fade into the light of common day. During these years men and women establish themselves on one of several levels: (1) the failures, who fall behind in the swift-moving procession and "lose out," financially, socially, often morally and spiritually; (2) the plodders, who fit their lives into a routine, as they do much the same thing in the same way month after month and year after year; (3) the thinkers, who look ahead, plan ahead, discover what at least they think they want for happiness, and move steadily toward it; (4) the doers, who, with initiative and aggressiveness, take the lead in accomplishing what they think ought to be done, and are usually thought of as the successful, "leading" men and women of a community. Take your church membership roll and select at random fifty men and women whom you know fairly well. Into which of these four classes would you place each of them? What are your conclusions?

These years of twenty-five to forty are years of achievement, but there may be the achievement of failure, of unhappiness, of chronic pessimism, of narrow selfishness, of worldly materialism. What is life's great need during these significant years? The answer can be given in one word—*Christ.* He can give life motive and direction, turn it into channels of usefulness and happiness and sustain it in the midst of trials and temptations. An unspeakably great ministry may be rendered by an adult Sunday school department and class to men and women who need supremely the spiritual stimulation and guidance which come from the study of God's Word, fresh contacts with Christ and fellowship in Christian service.

2. *Middle Life, the Period of Burden Bearing*

When Jesus cried, "Come unto me, all ye that labor and are heavy laden, and I will give you rest!" he may well have been speaking to a crowd of middle-aged adults. From forty to sixty the burdens of life tend to multiply. If a man is unsuccessful at forty, the burden of his failure rests heavily upon him and the chances of surmounting his difficulties and wresting victory out of defeat become increasingly remote. If he is successful, responsibility rests upon his shoulders as a load that grows heavier from year to year. For the woman past forty changes take place that bring weighty consequences. Often there is a serious disturbance of health. She may have thought that the children were a burden when they were young, but the sense of concern for them becomes almost overwhelming as she sees them reach maturity, leave the home nest, and go out into the world for themselves. To both men and women there comes, sometimes with a shock, the realization that by fifty they are no longer young, and have but a limited time left in which to accomplish their life purposes.

How do men and women, during this period of middle age, meet life's problems and carry life's burdens? There are some who break down completely. The demands made upon them are too heavy to bear, and they escape in many ways. Some collapse physically, and go down to early graves. Others suffer a nervous or mental breakdown, and become incapable of self-direction. Still others go to pieces morally. It is a matter of common observance that middle life witnesses the wreckage of character in men and women who hitherto had apparently lived irreproachable lives.

Fortunately for many the anchor holds. They have found safe harbor in Christ, and the storms of life cannot move them. They have accepted his offer, and in him have found peace and rest. In his service the yoke becomes easy and the burden light. They have learned the difference between the essential and the non-essential; they have discovered the uselessness of doubt and anxiety; they have learned how to conserve their energies and utilize their time; they are looking serenely to the joys of a life beyond this life. For them, life at its best has just begun.

Is it not clear that a Sunday school class may be made to meet fundamental needs of men and women during this burden-bearing period of life? To no other adult organization are given such possibilities. Has your class caught the vision of its power and usefulness in thus serving men and women who are in grave danger of being overborne unless they receive such help?

3. *Old Age, Life's Testing Time* Over 60

It is difficult to draw a line and say that past it one has become "old." Age is not altogether a matter of the calendar. Some people are older in spirit at fifty than others are at seventy. Usually, however, we think of a person as having got into the noble company of "old people" who has passed three score years. Almost certainly at this time vital powers begin to decline. Bodily strength is wasted faster than nature can build it up, and there is a general decline in physical and nervous vigor. In these final years life is put to the test. Shall it be spent in the shadows or in the sunshine? Shall it be a time of defeat or of victory?

Select a group of men and women sixty and above, and observe how they are meeting the tests of old age. Here are some who seem to be utterly miserable. They dwell continually on their aches and pains. They are cross, irritable, hard to please, always complaining, never satisfied. They find fault with everybody and everything and object to all that is new and different. They live in an idealized past, and can talk about little save the "good old days" which are now gone forever. Some have ruled God and the things of the Spirit out of their lives and have nothing left to live for. To some the approaching fact of death brings only horror, and they cling to the remnants of life with pathetic eagerness. Is there anything quite so distressing as bitter old age?

On the other hand, there are many old men and women, who like a sound apple, are mellowest and sweetest just before they drop from the bough. They have invested wisely and well their youth, their years of early maturity, their middle age. Now they are reaping the well-earned dividends of their investment. They have used their talents well for Christ, and now they can almost hear him say, "Well done . . . enter thou into the joy of thy Lord."

What can be done to help people who are growing old to meet the tests which come with infirmities and declining strength? How may the years be sweetened that might otherwise become bitter, and the sting be taken out of senescence? How can men and women, as they grow older, be made to feel that they are still useful and wanted, and their lives filled with joy instead of sadness? To the answering of these questions every Adult department should set itself, never forgetting that life is as precious in old age as in youth, and that one of the bitterest griefs of old age is the sense of being neglected and forgotten. Along with this responsibility is the golden opportunity of utilizing the ripe Christian experience, the mature wisdom and judgment, of these older Christians in solving the problems and meeting the spiritual needs of the younger groups. There are precious insights into the Word of God and inspiring experiences in the service of Christ which these older Christians can share with the younger. Often they can win to Christ those whom no one else can reach, because of the assurance with which they can speak, as they testify to his saving and keeping power. When regular attendance is no longer possible, the department should keep up its contacts with these aged saints, co-operating with the Extension department in making them to feel that they "still belong," and are not ignored and forgotten. To what extent is your department or class fulfilling its duty and privilege to the older people of the church and community?

4. *The Importance of Individual Differences*

We are born as individuals, we are saved as individuals, we die as individuals, and are judged as individuals. Our lives are intertwined with others in social groups, but we must never lose sight of our individual character and responsibility. We have much in common with others on the various levels of growth, but our individual differences are greater than our group like-

Don't teach a class — teach individuals —

nesses. Religion is a deeply personal matter and cannot be dispensed in wholesale lots. It is a mistake to think of people in terms of "classes," and to try to deal with them for religious purposes as if they were all alike.

The principle of division into age groups is a wise one, because it puts together those who have interests and needs in common, and who can thus think and work best together. But after the class divisions have been made, each class consists of individuals, every one of whom has a different history, different impulses and desires, different ideals and standards, different capacities and needs, different avenues of approach. It is of fundamental importance that class and department officers, and especially teachers, should recognize these needs and study them with utmost care. Only thus can we hope to reach and teach successfully the multitudes of adults who constitute the Sunday school's greatest challenge both in numbers and in possibilities of enlistment for Christ.

5. *Our Changed and Changing Adult World*

It requires no argument to prove that ours is a changed and changing world. Children born into these changed conditions do not feel the shock so severely as adults, who must somehow adjust themselves to the new order. Unquestionably the adults of this generation have witnessed one of the great turning points of history. What are some of the changed conditions which test the courage and stamina of adults today?

Consider *changes in the industrial system*. With amazing ingenuity men have perfected machines which do what in all other ages human hands were required to do. A machine, with one man to tend it, doing the work of ten men, puts nine men out of a job. These unemployed men cannot consume the products of the factories that have discharged them. The factories in turn must shut down. This in turn affects the demand for all sorts of raw materials and food stuffs. Thus, in large measure, we may account for the periodic "depressions" which bring the economic disaster with which we are sadly familiar.

The consequences of all this are grave and perilous, not only for our material welfare, but also for our religious well-being. Class-consciousness and strife become acute. The struggle for existence on the part of millions of unemployed releases the baser elements of self-preservation. Enforced idleness on the part of multitudes makes for disintegration of personality and loss of self-respect. Shorter hours of labor bring leisure beyond ability to employ it fruitfully. Our generation of adults faces almost unprecedented problems that have arisen out of the vast changes taking place in commerce and in industry.

Again, think of *changes in the social order*. The older forms of government are being discarded, and strange political theories are challenging the establishd order. The individual tends to be lost sight of in the crowd. For an increasing number, life is standardized and regimented. We must get to work at a given time, work a minimum number of hours for a fixed wage, and quit on the stroke of the clock. We go home in automobiles built according to standardized specifications, to apartments built so much alike that they can be told apart only by number, where we sit down to meals prepared at the delicatessen and bakery. We then read the newspaper containing exactly the same news as every other daily, and go to the theatre where we are amused by pictures that are released simultaneously throughout the nation, or listen to chain programs over the radio. We are treated for our ills at a clinic, die in the hospital ward, are buried by an authorized undertaker, in a funeral service that has been thoroughly standardized as to scripture, hymns, and remarks!

It is not easy for old-fashioned adults to get used to all this. Try as bravely as we will, do we not find ourselves a bit confused and upset by social conditions that have thrust us into a new world? We cannot understand adult life, with its perplexities and frequent breakdowns, if we do not take into account the pressure which has come from living in social conditions that are revolutionary.

Then, too, bear in mind *changes in religious thought and life*. The adults of today were for the most part brought up in communities where Sunday was looked upon as a day of rest and worship. Church and Sunday school attendance, for the majority, was taken for granted. There were no Sunday movies, no commercialized sports, few automobiles and almost no good roads, the Sunday newspaper was a rarity and the radio had not appeared. The churches had very little competition. Life was far from being ideally Christian, to be sure, but as children the adults of today were pretty generally taught to respect the church, reverence the Bible, and take religion seriously.

In contrast, we find all about us adults and young people alike who have lost the sense of moral conviction and certainty. What is right? What is wrong? We once knew the answer. For many now the distinction is no longer clear, and right and wrong blend hazily into each other. Right is what works, they say. Wrong is what fails to get quick results. We are all creatures of heredity and environment, the behaviorists declare. It follows, according to this reasoning, that we are not morally accountable for our character and conduct; sin is a theological fiction, and righteousness is purely a matter of social relationships. The sabbath for a multitude has ceased to be a holy day, the Bible has lost its authority, the church is an outworn institution, Christianity is a mixture of tradition and superstition. These are not the attitudes and opinions of callow youth merely, but of more mature men and women than we are perhaps willing to admit. It is profoundly important that these changes in the religious life and thought of modern adults be recognized and dealt with successfully.

6. *Making the Most of Adulthood*

Sometimes we talk as if the happiness and well-being of adults were of little importance. Children and young people, of course, have the right of joyous self-realization; but why should we bother about adults? They exist as means to the ends of the younger generation! In a sense this may be true, but we must never forget that the life of any person, young or old, is an end in itself. The happiness of a woman of seventy is just as precious a thing as the happiness of a maiden of seventeen. A man in the latter years of his life has just as much right to the joy of living as a young fellow just getting started. In the midst of all the changes and complexities which we have noticed, how may men and women of today make the most of adulthood? Three pathways to lasting satisfactions are suggested:

(1) *Through adjustment to new conditions*—It is a mistake to be forever fighting against the changes which are taking place about us. While some of these changes are to be deplored, some of them are for the better. Even when conditions are wrong, nothing is to be gained by growing cynical and bitter. Youth must have the leadership and wisdom of maturity if evils are to be overcome and wrongs righted. True wisdom lies in reconciliation to the inevitable, while facing with courage and determination conditions that can be changed. Would we go back to the horse and buggy days if we could? Would we have the young people of today exactly like we were if we might? May not God be preparing us for a fairer and better world, and may not the best era of the world's history be just ahead? One of life's best secrets is that of making satisfactory adjustments from stage to stage to one's growth and from development to development in the world about us.

(2) *Through the expansion of interests*—Life is worth most to him whose interests are broadest. The poorest individual is one who has the narrowest outlook and the fewest friends. True riches consist of an expanding

horizon, an ever enlarging circle of ideals, purposes, concerns. Never in all history has the world held out such possibilities of new and interesting experiences, of rich and worth-while contacts. The title of a popular book emphasizes this thought: "Life Begins at Forty." If life begins at forty, it ought by eighty to have drawn a circle about the universe, and put within this circle enough of experience and wisdom for a good beginning in eternity.

One of the differences between people is that for some life moves in a series of concentric circles that move inward toward a point. Such people, as they grow older, become more and more useless and dissatisfied. For others, life moves ever outward in constantly enlarging circles that include all that one brief span of years can gather. Think of certain men and women who represent the former type and others who represent the latter. Can you doubt who are making the most of their adulthood?

(3) *Through finding and following the will of God—* A great preacher once declared that every life is a plan of God. This does not mean that every life fulfils God's plan, for God has made us free creatures, and we may spoil the design if we will. We stress the necessity for children and young people discovering God's will for their lives, but do we not almost assume that adults have passed the necessity or possibility of this discovery? God's will for a life is progressive, and must be progressively revealed. There are new aspects of the divine purpose for a life as it moves onward from childhood to youth, from youth to manhood and womanhood, from the meridian of life to its sunset.

"Grow old along with me," Browning sang, "the best is yet to be!" But God's best is for those whose wills are attuned to his, who are in vital union with Christ as the branches with the vine. One who has thus found and followed God's way may with utmost confidence approach the end of the journey, able to say with Paul: "For I am now ready to be offered, and the time of my departure is at hand. I have fought a good fight, I have finished my course, I have kept the faith. Henceforth there is laid up for me a crown of righteousneses, which the Lord, the righteous judge, shall give me at that day: and not to me only, but unto all them also that love his appearing."

An essential part of the equipment of the teacher of adults is a vivid imagination. In every member of the class is a story of absorbing interest. From Sunday to Sunday, from year to year, the story is marked, "To be continued." Do you, as teacher, see your class as a mass, or as growing, changing individuals? Jesus said to his class of twelve men, "Come ye after me and I will make you become. . . ." This is your great business—to help a group of men and women to become, from stage to stage, what Christ wants them to be. What a glorious privilege and responsibility!

AIDS TO LEARNING

1. How many classes of adults are there in your Sunday school? Could there be more classes to advantage?

2. Why may the years forty to sixty be well called the period of burden bearing? Name some of the responsibilities that rest heavily upon men and women at this age. How may a Sunday school class help them?

3. When does a person become "old"? Name some of the marks of senescence that begin to be noticeable past sixty.

4. What are some of the handicaps of increasing years? What are some of the advantages?

5. Are there as wide differences between a junior of ten and a young person of twenty as between an adult of thirty and an adult of sixty? What are the consequences of putting adults thus widely separated in age in the same class? What should be done about it?

6. Discuss at least three ways in which modern men and women may make the most of adult life. Which one of these seems to you to have greatest practical value?

Teaching An Adult Class is
1. Not easy
2. Not all done on Sunday
3. Demanding on time
4. A matter of guiding individuals

THE ADULT TEACHER'S RESPONSIBILITY

OUTLINE

1. The Teacher's Personal Responsibility
2. The Teacher's Social Responsibility
3. The Teacher's Intellectual Responsibility
4. The Teacher's Spiritual Responsibility
5. The Teacher's High Calling

As we grow older, life brings to us increasing responsibilities. The more we have to do, the less energy we have with which to do it, as the years advance. The teaching of a Sunday school class makes heavy demands upon time and strength. Why accept this additional responsibility? "Get somebody else!" is the almost invariable response of the busy, capable adult when approached with the proposal to teach a class. Sometimes the appeal is made that teaching an adult class is not much of a task, after all. All one has to do, it is urged, is to get up a talk on the lesson, or ask questions from the *quarterly*, or provoke and direct a discussion. An hour's study on Saturday night, with a few minutes' fresh preparation on Sunday morning, will suffice! Nobody studies the lesson anyhow, and any one who is a fairly good talker and knows how to handle people can teach an adult Sunday school class! Have you ever heard this sort of argument? Have you known adult teachers who seemed to take this view of their responsibility?

Within recent years there has come a new conception of the adult Sunday school teacher's responsibility. This has been due in part to our advancing standards of teaching, and in part to the widespread movement for adult education. We are awakening to the importance of the Sunday school class as an educational agency, and of the teacher of adults as an educator of high rank. Let us look at the adult teacher's many-sided responsibility.

1. *The Teacher's Personal Responsibility*

Religion is a deeply personal matter. It involves a personal relationship to God through Christ, personal beliefs and standards, personal attitudes towards others, a personal code of conduct. Religion is not something that can be taught as a system of abstract truths—it must rather be caught through the contagion of personal contacts. The teacher of religion must himself be genuinely religious. It is a great hour in the life of a Sunday school teacher when he or she can say, "I myself am the most important human factor in the success or failure of my teaching." This is not egotism; it is the frank recognition that divine truth must have human channels, and that the teacher is, next to the preacher, the most important channel through which the truth of God is made available to the minds and hearts of men.

The teacher's first responsibility is to see that the channel between himself and God is kept open. It is easy for the channel to become clogged by absorption in selfish interests, by compromise with the world, by neglect of prayer, by wrong motives and purposes, by harsh and ungenerous attitudes toward others, by pessimism and discouragement, by doubt and false belief. It is not easy to live up to the standards which we profess and teach. It is difficult to be a genuine Christian in the midst of life's trials and disappointments. Sometimes God seems afar off, Christ but a name, and the Holy Spirit just a figure of speech. How can the teacher keep his heart warm, his love for Christ glowing, his devotion to his task a living thing?

(1) *There must be a new nature.* Jesus demanded of Nicodemus, a learned teacher and a morally upright man, that he be "born again" before he could enter into the

kingdom of God. This new birth comes from a sincere turning away from the love of sin, and a whole-hearted acceptance of Jesus Christ as Saviour and Lord. When this is done *something happens,* through the operation of the Holy Spirit, and thereafter there is a new nature, a changed mind, a transformed life. No teacher can teach spiritual truth as revealed in the Scriptures who has not had this experience.

(2) *There must be a great love.* Paul declared the secret when he said, "The love of Christ constrains us." From the beginning Christians have closed their prayers with the words, "For Jesus' sake." Why do teachers undertake to teach? Sometimes because they are over-persuaded, although their hearts are not in it. Sometimes because it gives a sense of personal satisfaction. Sometimes the urge is that of duty, a feeling of obligation because there is no one else to do it. Much failure in teaching may be accounted for by these insufficient motives.

The true Sunday school teacher must be willing to say, "I recognize my weaknesses and limitations. I realize that teaching is not easy, and I must pay the price of success. But if my church wants me for this service, and the Holy Spirit has impressed me that I should do it, I will gladly do my best for Jesus' sake." The teacher who has made this dedication ceases to be moved by the praise or criticism of others, and is undiscouraged by problems and difficulties. Such a teacher is not working for men but for the Master, and is able to say with Paul, "But far be it from me to glory, save in the cross of our Lord Jesus Christ, through which the world hath been crucified unto me, and I unto the world." Have you, as a teacher, made this dedication?

(3) *There must be high purpose.* The teacher without purpose is doomed to failure. It is not enough to be willing to teach. There must be active, enthusiastic determination. It is doubtful if God wants us to render service to him of compulsion and constraint. Surely he

wants us to be happy in our work. A teacher without purpose is bound to be an ineffective, unhappy teacher. Ask a dozen teachers of adult classes, "What is your chief purpose in teaching?" and note the answers. Sadly enough, some will look blank and confess that they do not know how to express their highest purpose.

The teacher's purpose will, of course, depend somewhat upon circumstances, and will vary with different situations and individuals. The supremely important matter is that there shall be a high purpose, and that this purpose shall be kept steadily in view. Jesus, when asked to name the first and greatest commandment, replied, "Thou shalt love the Lord thy God . . . and thy neighbor as thyself." May we not re-state our purpose as teachers in terms of whole-hearted love to God and unselfish devotion to the welfare of others?

2. *The Teacher's Social Responsibility*

It is literally true that no man lives to himself nor dies to himself. We are all bound up in the bundle of humanity, and we cannot escape responsibility for others if we would. By nature we are social beings. Christianity is a religion of social as well as personal relationships. The Sunday school teacher is not only a transmitter of ideas but an influencer of human lives. The impact of his life upon the lives of members of his class is often more formative than the words which he speaks in the presentation of the lesson. How can the teacher of adults discharge this grave social responsibility?

(1) *There must be genuine love of people.* The first requirement for helping another is to convince him of your friendly interest. If this friendly interest can then be deepened into real love there are almost endless possibilities of helpfulness. Love, in this high Christian sense, is the outgoing of desire for another's welfare, together with the determination to do something to promote the happiness and well-being of the one thus loved. It is easy to love some people, but difficult to love others.

How can the teacher cultivate a loving disposition toward all sorts of people—the unlovely as well as the lovable, the repugnant as well as the attractive, the sinner as well as the saint?

This fixed attitude of love toward all men comes about, first, through a constant reminder of God's love in Christ for all. God so loved *the world* that he gave his Son; and Christ so loved the whole of humanity that he died that *whosoever* will may have his salvation. The teacher must constantly say, "If God can love this person, I can." Again, love is the result of deepened understanding and appreciation. If a teacher has the spirit of Christ, and knows the struggles, temptations, disappointments, hardships, weaknesses, and misfortunes of another, he is bound to have compassion on him. He will hate his sin, but he must love the sinner, if the mind is in him that was in Christ. No man or woman is truly fitted to teach a Sunday school class who has not learned this fundamental secret of compassionate yearning over people and longing to help them.

(2) *There must be generous sharing of oneself and one's substance.* Christianity is a religion of shared values. Indeed, it makes the true test of any value the extent to which it can be shared. When property or money ceases to be sharable it ceases to be valuable. The same is true of ideas—they become worthless if not passed on to others. The principal holds good especially in the realm of the spiritual—if we do not share with others our soul experiences they grow cold and lifeless. How can the teacher fulfil this obligation?

The sharer must have something to share. Peter could say, "Silver and gold have I none, but such as I have I give." The teacher must have a genuine Christian experience, and this experience must be kept fresh and vital. Whatever separates from God's approval and the sense of Christ's living presence must be avoided; and spiritual fires must be kept burning through daily Bible study, meditation and prayer, attendance on public worship, and unselfish service.

1. Keep full of something worth sharing
2. Be the kind of person that has much in his life worth sharing

The point at which the teacher can make the richest contribution, however, is in the sharing of *himself*. Nearly all of us repress too much our personal religious emotions, thus creating an atmosphere in which members of the class dare not express what is most on their hearts. Do you really love God? Is Christ a present reality who walks and talks with you? Has the Holy Spirit manifested his comforting and guiding power to you? Have you tried Christ's way of life and found it true? Then make your teaching glow with the light of these experiences! You will never know the highest joy of teaching until you have got away from abstractions and learned the art of sharing yourself with your class, and leading them to share themselves with you and with one another.

(3) *There must be acceptance of responsibility for one's influence.* The teacher of a Sunday school class, as the minister of a church, is no longer a private individual. The church has placed the teacher, alongside the pastor, in an office of great importance. The teacher is the representative of Christ and the church, not only on Sunday, but throughout the week. Paul announced the guiding principle of the teacher when he said that he would eat no meat—even though he had the right to do it—if by so doing he caused his brother to stumble. In what ways especially must the teacher guard this responsibility for his influence?

First, *by positive, consistent Christian living.* Every teacher teaches more effectively by what he is and does than by what he says. When a man undertakes to say one thing out of one corner of his mouth, and something else out of the other, the result is—nothing. When his tongue speaks one language and his life another, we have no difficulty in knowing which to believe. One of the sorriest of all spectacles is that of a teacher—or preacher—whose deeds give the lie to his doctrine. Better a teacher whose teaching is in stammering words but whose life is true to Christ than the most brilliant scholar whose walk contradicts his talk.

2. Negatively, the teacher's responsibility extends to *the avoidance of every appearance of evil.* There are many things which seem to be on the borderline between good and evil. What course shall the good teacher pursue? A good rule is, "When in doubt, take the safe side." Shall the Sunday school teacher play cards, engage in dancing, go to places of questionable amusements, participate in unethical business or professional practices, take the unchristian side in social and political issues? The answer is an emphatic "No," if he would maintain the sanctity of his influence.

3. Again, *the teacher's influence depends largely upon his loyalties.* To what do you give your first allegiance? *what comes first?* Paul could say, "For to me to live is Christ and to die is gain." Can you? True loyalty to Christ will express itself in loyalty to his Kingdom, his church, his Word, his work. If you are a teacher, is there any position which you hold or any task committed to your hands which should take priority? You may have a fine sense of loyalty to your family, to your job, to your friends, and yet be sadly lacking in a sense of loyalty to your class. The teacher who lacks this loyalty will never attain the highest success. How can a teacher get his consent to be absent on Sunday without having made provision for some one to take his place? How can his conscience permit him to put a bit of indisposition, or a business matter, or a pleasure trip, ahead of his duty as a teacher? Yet the tragic fact is that many do these very things—and then wonder why they have so little influence!

3. *The Teacher's Intellectual Responsibility*

Teaching and learning are mental operations. Human beings are taught; animals can only be trained. In human learning mind reacts to mind, and without such impact of mind upon mind our development as normal human beings would be impossible. Heavy responsibility rests, therefore, upon the teacher for providing the

teacher must want + be willing to learn

best possible intellectual equipment for his task, and for the stimulation and use of the mental powers of the class. What are some of the most important phases of the teacher's intellectual responsibilty?

(1) *The teacher should be an unceasing student of the Bible.* The Bible has been called the textbook of the Sunday school. It is far more than that. It is the living Word of God. It is life-giving Truth, to be had nowhere else. The Scriptures are to the spiritual nature of man what food and drink are to the physical. The soul starves that does not feed on the Bible. Have you not noticed this difference between two teachers—one teaches from the overflow of a soul that is full and abundant, while the other painfully struggles to teach a "lesson" beyond which he dare not go? Let us see what it takes to make one a "fountain of living waters" rather than a dry well in teaching:

Let the Bible be recognized as the source of spiritual authority. _not his own ideas_ The Sunday school teacher is not to teach ideas of his own devising. It is not his business to lecture on science and art and philosophy—or even on religion. He is not set for the defense of peculiar "isms" nor for the overthrow of social and political theories. He must, of course, deal with the great issues of life, but always in the light of divine truth as revealed in the Book. Questions concerning all sorts of problems will arise, but they are to be solved not by human wisdom but by appeal to the one source of ultimate wisdom —the Bible. This becomes the teacher's supreme intellectual responsibility—to discover in God's Word the answer to life's questions and the solution of life's problems.

Let the Bible be studied as a whole, not merely as unrelated parts. The Bible is a unity, not just a collection of sixty-six books. It has its beginning in the tragic story of man's sin; its unfoldment of God's redemptive purpose in the history, poetry, and prophecy of the Old Testament; its climax in the birth, life, teachings, death, and resurrection of Jesus Christ; its fulfilment in the record of the growth of Christianity and the interpretation of Christ and his salvation; its culmination in the picture and promise of final victory when the kingdoms of this world shall have become the kingdom of our Lord and of his Christ, who shall reign forever. The teacher who brings to his class little fragments of the Bible, set off from the Book as a whole and unrelated to the total purpose of Christ and to present life, is cheating his class of their God-given right.

Let the Bible be interpreted in the light of modern conditions. The Bible is both a timeless and a timely Book. It is timeless in that its great truths apply to every age and condition. It is timely in that these truths must be selected and interpreted to meet changing needs and situations. The Bible throws the light of the past on the pathway of the present and the future in order that we may have safe guidance for life's journey. Its great truths, summarized in certain familiar passages, are not to be thought of as isolated texts, or memory verses, but must be studied in their context if understood and appreciated. A teacher who puts biblical facts in a framed "outline" and then holds up the picture to the class for a half-hour, making no vital connection with present life, has missed the work of real teaching.

(2) *The teacher should be a diligent student of human life.* Jesus said, "I am come that ye might have life." He did not teach "lessons" from a textbook, but drew his truths from life. It is said of him that "He knew what was in man." The Sunday school teacher, accepting Jesus as the Master Teacher, should likewise make his teaching life-centered, and therefore should seek to understand those whom he would teach. How?

By mingling much with people. The critics of Jesus murmured against him because he companied and ate with sinners. Jesus was no remote Teacher who kept aloof from the people and appeared occasionally to give a discourse. He was constantly the center of a crowd. Observe the many occasions when small groups and great multitudes gathered about him. In this he has set the example for us as teachers. No teacher can fulfil his mission whose contacts with his class are limited to the Sunday session. To know men and women the teacher must go where they are, watch them at work and play, and mingle with them on terms of easy and cordial equality.

By singling out individuals for special study. It is not enough to know people *en masse.* A crowd or a class is made up of individuals. No two individuals in all the world are exactly alike. What can be more fascinating than to take a Sunday school class roll and make a thoughtful study of each person represented? Take a given case—Mr. A., let us say. How old is he? Where does he live? Is he married or single? How many in his family? What does he do for a living? Is his education above or below average? Is he quick or slow in his responses? Is he self-confident and aggressive or timid and shy? Is he a Christian? An active church member? Are his moral standards high or low? Is he spiritually minded or worldly? Is his interest in Bible study incidental and superficial or sustained and real? Is he faithful and regular in church and Sunday school attendance, or careless and irregular? Does he appear to be happy and contented, or worried and dissatisfied? Is he really getting anything out of his connection with the class, or does he attend from habit, or sense of duty, or persuasion? How close have you as teacher come to his inner life? What stands between him and you to prevent a heart-to-heart understanding and friendship? How can any apparent barrier to such a fellowship be removed? Think of what it would mean if a teacher should thus prayerfully and intelligently set himself to know every individual in the class!

The teacher should keep abreast of best methods. Methods of teaching, of class and department organization, of winning and holding adults, are constantly being improved. The teacher's responsibility reaches beyond that of classrooom instruction and personal contacts. An adult class rarely functions as a successful outreaching and serving agency if the teacher has no interest in this aspect of its work. Class officers look to the teacher for encouragement and guidance. Time for reports must be gladly given by the teacher or they will cease to be made. If the teacher does not think the records are important no one else will. The teacher's spirit, more than anything else, will determine the degree of co-operation and loyalty of the class in its relation to the department, the school, and the church. It is as inexcusable for a teacher to fall into the rut of using the same method of teaching as it would be for a cook to serve exactly the same meal month after month. Shall we not agree that the teacher owes an inescapable obligation to the class to keep abreast of the best modern methods?

4. *The Teacher's Spiritual Responsibility*

The crowning service of the Sunday school teacher is spiritual. Others may share responsibility for personal influence, for social enrichment, and for intellectual guidance; but the teacher of a Sunday school class is a specialist in the field of spiritual nurture. We close our study by a brief look at this supremely important phase of the teacher's commission.

(1) *Make clear the meaning of true spirituality.* There is a vast lot of misunderstanding as to the meaning and expression of "spirituality." Some confuse it with religious emotionalism. Others think that it is a species of other-worldliness that ignores all the commonplace facts of life. Still others view it as the rare gift of the Spirit to a few fortunate souls who are out of the class of ordinary beings.

The New Testament conception of spirituality is far different from all of these mistaken ideas. True spir-

ituality is the result of opening one's mind to the Holy
Spirit's guidance, and surrendering oneself to his leadership and power. The disciples were never more spiritual than when, at Pentecost, they were endued by the
Holy Spirit with power for effectual witness. There are,
Paul explains, two ways of life—to be led by the Spirit,
or to be controlled by the desires of the flesh. The op-
posite of spirituality is selfishness. To put Christ and
others at the center, and self in the circumference, is to
be spiritual in the New Testament sense. To know
Christ, to love him, and to make it the chief purpose of
one's life to bring others to know and to love him, is the
essence of genuine spirituality.

(2) *Keep the spiritual dominant.* There are two
claimants for the right to control our lives—Christ and
self. Almost every waking hour of one's life the claims
of Christ and of self are in conflict. Which shall gain
and hold the supremacy? The teacher who has not answered this question satisfactorily in his own life will
find it difficult if not impossible to help others to answer
it.

Perhaps the greatest single cause of spiritual weakness
and of unrest and discontent is double-mindedness. In
a half-hearted way most of us want to be worthy Christians. But for many the call of the world drowns out
the call of the Spirit. On Sunday we respond to the
Christian ideal; but during the week we compromise by
yielding to the standard of the world. The secret of spiritual power is whole-hearted committal to Christ and
his way of life—the singleness of purpose which our
Lord taught, and which Paul and all great Christians
have found to be the only path to usefulness and joy.
Few responsibilities of the teacher are greater that that
of making this the dominant note in all that is said and
done.

(3) *Harness spiritual forces to everyday tasks.* Religion, for many adults, has lost its appeal because it seems
to have so little bearing on the ordinary affairs of life.

They are surrounded by the problems of making a living, rearing children, getting along with the neighbors, meeting social demands, and the like. What has religion to do with all these commonplace activities? If the teacher does not show that what he teaches, and what the class stands for, is of primary practical value in the ordinary affairs of life, he will fail in one of his highest responsibilities.

Christ revealed that religion is not a thing apart from life, but *life itself*. When the Christian motive is dominant there are no longer any ordinary, secular affairs. All of life's interests and activities become sacred, because life is a divine-human partnership, lived under the will of God for the purposes of Jesus Christ. Making money, the day's work, the cares of the household, being a good neighbor, enjoying life's good things, meeting life's disappointments and sorrows—all of the ordinary affairs of daily living—take on new meaning when motivated by the love of God in Christ and guided by the Holy Spirit. Let a Sunday school class make real and vital this conception of religion, and harness the spiritual power of Christian teaching and fellowship to everyday affairs, and men and women will rise up to call it blessed.

5. *The Teacher's High Calling*

As you contemplate these grave responsibilities of the Sunday school teacher—personal, social, intellectual, spiritual—does your heart grow faint within you? Are you tempted to cry, "Who is sufficient for these things?" The object of this study will have been defeated if you view your responsibility with a sense of helplessness and defeat. We dare not face the demands made upon us in our own strength and wisdom. Let us, then in deep humility, but in calm confidence, make ours these great words of Paul's: "For behold your calling, brethren; that not many wise after the flesh, not many mighty, not many noble, are called: but God chose the foolish things of the world, that he might put to shame them that are wise; and God chose the weak things of the world, that

1. Yes, the Adult teacher should have all these qualities
2. Don't face this with despondency
3. Depend on God to supply

he might put to shame the things that are strong; and the base things of the world, and the things that are despised, did God choose, yea and the things that are not, that he might bring to nought the things that are: that no flesh should glory before God. But of him are ye in Christ Jesus, who was made unto us wisdom from God, and righteousness and sanctification, and redemption: that, according as it is written, He that glorieth, let him glory in the Lord."

AIDS TO LEARNING

1. Suppose you were delegated to interview a capable man or woman with a view to getting his or her consent to teach an adult Sunday school class. What wrong arguments would you avoid? What valid appeal would you make?

2. Why is the teacher's first responsibility that of maintaining right personal relations with God? How may the channel between the teacher and God be clogged? How may it be kept open?

3. What is meant by the statement, "By nature we are social beings"? Why is the social life of the teacher of fundamental importance?

4. Which is more important, for the teacher to share with the class his knowledge or himself? What is necessary before the teacher can thus share himself with others?

5. Which is greater, the teacher's direct or indirect influence— what he says or what he is? What must the teacher avoid if he would maintain his influence?

6. Why is the teacher's spiritual responsibility paramount? How is the teacher to discharge this supreme obligation? What follows if the teacher does not keep the spiritual uppermost?

Animal life is simple — needs can be cared for by Nature
Man is complex — takes: 1. Nature
2. God
3. Society

God has given a Book of Guidance — Bible
God's Book — Over 2 Billion Copies printed since
John Gutenberg printed the 1st.
Billy Sunday on the Bible

CHAPTER V

MEETING ADULT NEEDS WITH THE BIBLE

OUTLINE

1. The Trunk-Line Problems of Adults

2. The Need of a Personal Saviour

3. The Need of Religious Certainty

4. The Need of Sustaining Motives

5. The Need of Tested Standards

6. The Need of Practical Expression

From the cradle to the grave we humans are needy creatures. We are born dependent, and remain dependent all our lives. The human infant is the most helpless of all young, over the longest period of time. The enemies of human life are more numerous and more destructive than of any other form of life. The needs of animals are wholly physical, and are supplied by nature. The needs of men are physical, social, intellectual, and spiritual, and must be supplied not only by nature but by society and God. Animal life begins at birth and ceases at death. Man is immortal. Between the highest animal and the lowest man there is an infinite gulf fixed because of differences in origin, capacities, interests, problems, possibilities, destiny.

How are these complex needs of human life to be supplied? Nature is certainly not a sufficient source of supply. Man, through his own wisdom, is incapable of meeting his immeasurable needs. Man's needs are infinite, hence must have an infinite source of supply. This source is God, who made man in his own image. Why should it be thought strange that God, who made man with capacities and needs that nature and reason cannot supply, should have given to him a Book from which to secure the guidance and help available nowhere else?

The Bible may well be described as a divinely inspired literature of experience, written in the language of experience, for the salvation, enrichment, and guidance of human life. The Bible is vastly more than history, poetry, oratory, prophecy, biography, doctrine. It makes use of these many literary forms, but they are means to the end of revealing God and his will for our lives, and showing us how to live so as to achieve the true ends of life. A teacher is at his best who faces life as it is, with all its problems and perplexities, and then with skill and insight helps those whom he teaches to find in the Bible the answers to life's deepest questions.

1. *The Trunk-Line Problems of Adults*

A "problem" is a felt need for which there is no ready-made supply. Some of our needs are supplied without much thought or effort on our part. We do not think of our need of air, or sunshine, or rain, or time, or space, or the normal functioning of our bodies and minds as problems. But when nature fails to act consistently, as in a drouth or an earthquake, or when physical or mental illness occurs, immediately problems arise. For most of us, life consists largely of one problem after another. Some of these problems are of major importance, some of minor importance. In this respect, life may be compared to a map on which are indicated multitudes of small roads that link up with trunk-line highways. A first step in meeting adult needs with the Bible is the location and statement of certain major problems that are common to us all. Such a listing of fundamental problems, somewhat in the order of their immediate pressure upon the average individual, would certainly include the following:

Personal health and happiness.
Family relationships.
Economic and social security.

Adults problems are varied - most are the same, but arranged & accentuated differently.

Congenial acquaintances and friends.
Leisure time activities.
Emotional outlets.
Intellectual satisfactions.
Avenues of self-expression.
Altruistic service. — *Unselfish Service to Others*
Divine approval.

Examine yourself. Which of these constitute for you felt difficulties? To which have you found the least satisfactory answers? How would you arrange this list in the order of importance for your life? Now take a dozen other adults—members of your Sunday school class—and consider which of these problems, in each case, seem to be most acute. Are you not made to realize, that, beginning with yourself, and extending to every adult you know, life is made up of problems for which the wisdom of God, the love of Christ, and the guidance of the Holy Spirit are absolutely necessary?

So, life is made up of problems

2. *The Need of a Personal Saviour*

One of the most difficult problems which any man faces is himself. When we turn our thoughts in upon ourselves, we are constrained to cry out with the Psalmist, "I am fearfully and wonderfully made!" Who can fully understand himself? Man's physical nature is the most complex organism known to science. Sociology is just beginning to reveal the complexities of human relationships. Psychology has made scarcely more than a good beginning in the study of mental complexities. Then when we realize how little we know about spiritual capacities and possibilities, we stand even more amazed at the universe within us than at the universe around us.

As we examine ourselves, we find that the most tragic fact concerning us is *sin*. We have deliberately broken the laws of God. We have misused life's highest gifts. We have lived meanly and selfishly. In the presence of what we knew to be the higher, we have chosen the lower. We have put our own wills above the will of

1. God made man wonderfully, but complex
2. God made man for his purposes
3. Man is a willfully sinful, proud creature
4. Man needs a personal Saviour - the Bible's Christ

God, and our own interests ahead of the interests of others. It is literally true that "all we like sheep have gone astray; we have turned every one to his own way." We stand guilty of the charge, "they are all gone out of the way, they are together become unprofitable; there is none that doeth good, no, not one." It is impossible to save ourselves, for we are "by nature children of wrath."

In the helplessness of his sin and guilt, man must have a savior. It is for this reason that God sent his Son into the world, not to condemn the world, but that the world should be saved through him. "He that believeth on him is not judged; he that believeth not has been judged already, because he has not believed on the name of the only begotten Son of God." The first and deepest of all human needs is that of salvation from sin and its consequences, and a new relationship to God that brings forgiveness, peace, and joy. This new life in God comes when Jesus Christ is accepted as personal Saviour, and made Lord and Master of one's life.

The Bible's supreme purpose is the meeting of this supreme need. The Bible is a Christ-centered book. Every chapter in the Old Testament gets its chief value from its service in preparing the way for Christ's coming. The Gospels are a portraiture of this divine-human Saviour, who lived, died, and rose again for our salvation. All the remaining books of the New Testament are an interpretation of Christ and his redemptive plan and power. Have you ever stopped to consider how hopeless humanity would be were it not for the fulfilment of this need of salvation through the Word of God?

3. *The Need of Religious Certainty*

The most certain thing about human life is its uncertainty. The wisest of men cannot know what a day will bring forth. We make our little plans, but a thousand unexpected circumstances upset them. We make much of logic, only to find that the things we do are far from sensible. We compliment ourselves on our freedom of thought and belief, but a bit of honest inquiry reveals that we think what we have been taught to think, and believe what has been handed down to us from the past. Why are you a Democrat, or a Republican, or a Baptist? Maybe you are one of the few who have thought it all through, and come to independent conclusions based on research and reason. If so, you are in position to render an inestimable service to those who have not reached this high ground.

Ours is an age of religious uncertainty. There are so many voices making contradictory claims that it is difficult to know whom to believe. Convictions once held as dear as life itself have lost their force for many. Science has boldly challenged theology, and in the wrestle of the scientist with the theologian the latter has not always seemed to come off victorious. The modern man or woman cannot read the newspapers and magazines, listen to the radio, attend popular lectures, and keep up with semi-scientific books without having serious questions raised as to religious fundamentals.

Get a mixed group of intelligent adults to discussing religion. What are some of the questions that will arise? Almost certainly they will be asking: Is there an objectively real, personal God? Did God make the universe, or did it come into existence apart from divine creation? Is the Bible the unique Word of God, or is it just a collection of valuable religious literature? Can we still believe in miracles, or may they be explained on natural grounds? Is faith in Christ the ony way of salvation, or can men be saved by character and good works? If God is a God of infinite power and wisdom, why is there so much evil in the world? If God is love, why is there so much suffering? What will become of those who have never had a chance to hear the gospel? Does God actually answer prayer, or do we answer our own prayers? Is there a real devil and an actual hell, or do these words represent figures of speech? How does the death of Christ alter the consequences of sin? Can the soul

4. Doubt has been raised to Many religious Assumptions
5. A Great problem is "How to apply religion"
6. The Bible is our answer to these problems

live apart from the body? What sort of existence will there be after death? When and how will Christ come again? How may we know the will of God for our lives? What is a church for, and what value has it for our day? Is Christianity the only true religion, or is it one of several true religions? Of the many Christian denominations, how may we know which one is right? When religious leaders disagree, how shall we know the truth? Can we today be Christians according to Christ?

Here are questions nearly every one of which would be debated in a mixed group of intelligent adults. Concerning every one of these questions, some would say one thing, some another. Even ministers would be divided on some of them. Is it any wonder that there should be a general sense of confusion in the minds of many thoughtful people?

The Bible stands as our unfailing source of certainty in answering these and similar questions. We do well to go back to a declaration of faith made by our Baptist fathers some two hundred years ago, when they, too, were faced with this problem of religious uncertainty. In the so-called "Philadelphia Confession of Faith," adopted by the Baptist Association which met at Philadelphia, September 25, 1742, it is declared: "We believe that the Holy Bible was written by men divinely inspired, and is a perfect treasure of heavenly instruction; that it has God for its author, salvation for its end, and truth, without any mixture of error, for its matter; that it reveals the principles by which God will judge us; and therefore is and shall remain to the end of the world the true center of Christian union, and the supreme standard by which all human conduct, creeds, and opinions should be tried." Shall we not reverently thank God that this convincing statement holds as good for our day as it did for the day of our fathers? What a world of doubt and confusion this would be, in the midst of our prevailing lack of religious certainty, were it not for the Word of God!

Animals driven by cravings — Humans by motives.

1. Behind most human actions are motives.

2. Too many motives are selfish

4. *The Need of Sustaining Motives*

Human life is distinguished by the presence of motives. Animals are driven by more or less blind instincts in response to their natural cravings. Human behavior is actuated by motives. We do some things through instinct and habit, but even then there are usually present certain unconscious motives. A motive, thus considered, is an intelligent, compelling urge toward a desired end. Sometimes a motive may be negative—the urge to avoid undesirable consequences. Sometimes the end sought is not in itself most desirable, but is the lesser of two evils, as when a man works cheerfully at a job he dislikes in order to earn money to buy something he really wants. Much failure and unhappiness are due to lack of right motives, or to confused motives. It is of the greatest importance that men and women possess strong, clearly defined, sustaining motives.

Get together a group of average adults and ask them, What are your motives? Why do you do what you do? What sustains you to keep on keeping on? The answers, if honestly given, will be interesting and revealing. Among the motives most often given will be: To maintain a home, to provide the necessities and comforts of life, to enjoy pleasures and luxuries, to guarantee future independence, to provide education and privileges for one's children, to achieve distinction and power, to gain the approval and good will of others, to be useful in service, to demonstrate love for Christ, to fulfil a sense of duty, to win eternal reward, to please God and gain his approval. Read this list of motives carefully. Which of them move you most powerfully? Which are selfish and which are unselfish? Which have you found to give most lasting satisfactions? Which are most truly Christian?

The test of a motive is this: does it move inward toward self, or outward toward God and others? Over and over the Bible enforces the lesson, out of all sorts of experiences of all kinds of men, that the selfish motive

3. The most rewarding motives are unselfish

4. Christian motives, from Bible, are unselfish

— are Vicarious

drives to selfish conduct, and selfish conduct is self-defeating. The only life worth living is a life whose ends lie outside of self, the achievement of those ends being motivated by love of God and love of others. Every time one opens the Bible one finds some fresh light thrown on that great revelation of Jesus, that whosoever would save his life shall lose it, but whosoever will lose his life, for Christ's sake and the gospel's, will save it. How incalculable is the value of the Bible in thus enabling us to discover, define, and utilize motives that alone can make life worthwhile!

5. *The Need of Tested Standards*

Life, to be stable, must have dependable standards. Is it not strange that, in a day when standards are rigidly applied to nearly everything else, standards of religious faith and moral conduct should be loose and uncertain? The application of precise standards has given us the modern world of scientific discovery. The telegraph, the telephone, the radio, the automobile, the airplane, the factory with its amazing machines, industry with its efficiency, the arts and sciences with their precision—all these pay their tribute to the principle of standardization. Yet men and women everywhere are groping in confusion concerning standards of right and wrong, of good and evil, of truth and error, of success and failure, of happiness and misery. What greater service could the teacher of an adult Sunday school class render than to bring those whom he teaches to clear, straight thinking concerning standards by which to measure belief and behaviour in these fundamentally important realms?

Engage a group of average adults in discussion concerning moral and spiritual standards. Ask them if a lie is ever justifiable; if it pays always to be honest; if impure thought is as wrong as impure action; if evading taxes is as bad as beating the grocery bill; if it is any worse to cheat one's neighbor than a great cor-

1. The whole business + social world operates on a standard
2. A religious + ethical standard is fuzzy today
3. Need for S.S. Teachers to have standard
4. " " " " to teach "

poration; if one can be a good citizen and yet neglect
to vote; if one can be a good church member and get
profit from some such evil as the liquor business; if
playing poker for money is any worse than playing
bridge for a prize; if one can be a consistent Christian
and yet engage in questionable amusements; if divorce
and remarriage are justifiable on any other grounds
than adultery; if fathers and mothers may do what they
forbid their children to do; if there is any difference between robbing God of his tithe and robbing one's neighbor; if Sunday is to be thought of chiefly as a holiday or
a day of rest and worship; if church obligations are any
less sacred than business obligations; if corrupt business
and political practices are one's personal concern, or to
be thought of as the other fellow's business.

Study these problems in Christian ethics. Are you
entirely clear on them all? Think of your Sunday school
class. Could you get unanimous agreement on these
moral issues? Where there is sharp difference of opinion,
how shall a decision be reached? Shall we accept some
man's opinion as authoritative? Shall we let the majority opinion rule? Shall we agree that each person
is to be a law unto himself? Clearly what we need are
standards backed up by divine authority. Such standards we have revealed in the Bible, which is the one
book given by God to men for this very purpose. Here
is a need, deep and universal, that can be met in no other
way than through the study of God's Word.

6. *The Need of Practical Expression*

It is a well recognized law that impression without expression leads to depression. Jesus compares the man
who hears but does not to one who built his house on a
foundation of sand. James admonishes us to be doers of
the word, and not hearers only. He further declares that
faith without works is dead. The majority of adults
know far better than they do. Conscience, providence,
history, experience, example, teaching, preaching, com-

1. Learn how to put faith into action
2. Learn discipline of life toward a goal
3. Apply every lesson & issue a challenge with suggestions as to how to do it.

bine to impress us with what we ought to do. The tragedy of many lives, however, is that they drift along from day to day, from year to year, in purposeless inactivity. We need to know how to budget our time, and then to be taught how to move steadily toward certain definite objectives.

A question which should be constantly uppermost in the mind of Bible class teacher, as he presents any truth, is: What are we going to do about it? Give this question concrete illustration in a particular adult class. Say to them: "We know that there are lost people around us; what are we going to do about it? We know that there are sick and needy in our community; what are we going to do about it? We know that there are unreached people who should be brought to our class; what are we going to do about it? We know that our church and denomination need more money with which to carry on the work of the Kingdom; what are we going to do about it? We know that there are evil influences surrounding our young people which should be removed; what are we going to do about it? We know that there are rotten spots in political, social, industrial conditions; what are we going to do about it? We know that we neglect prayer, Bible-study, worship; what are we going to do about it? We know that our lives are selfish and worldly; what are we going to do about it?"

Well, what are we going to do about it? Who has the right to tell us? How can we find out what can and ought to be done? God has not left us without light and guidance. The Bible never presents a duty without giving a corresponding course of conduct. None need grope in the dark as to what to do who will go earnestly and prayerfully to the Bible and seek diligently and intelligently for the answer. The glory of God's Word is that it says, "This is the way, walk ye in it."

No wonder the Bible has been called "the Book of books!" No wonder it continues to be the world's best seller! It is an old book, but it is also the newest of books. It is a book that grew out of the experiences of men with God in ancient times, but God remains the same and human need remains the same. The Bible therefore is as modern as the sun, as fresh as the morning dew, as life-giving as the air we breathe. So long as we need God, so long as we need salvation from sin, so long as we need religious certainty in the midst of human confusion, so long as we need motives that sustain us when all else fails, so long as we need moral and spiritual standards that will stand the test, so long as we need a way of life that will lead unerringly to the fulfilment of God's high purpose in Christ—so long as these needs remain, so long will the Bible be treasured as God's great revelation to man, imperishable and irreplaceable. Let us take our stand with Isaiah in the conviction that "the grass withereth, the flower fadeth, but the word of our God shall stand forever." In this conviction let us teach it and live it, in the absolute certainty that Jesus was right when he said, "Ye shall know the truth, and the truth shall make you free."

Have you, as a teacher of adults, made this twofold discovery—that every member of your class has deep and pressing needs, and that every need can find its supply in the Bible? If so you are now prepared to see your responsibility in this new light—that you must know the basic needs of every individual whom you would teach, and know how to find the supply of these fundamental needs in the Book you teach. Thus may you realize the ideal of Paul when he says that Christ gave some to be teachers, "for the perfecting of the saints, unto the work of ministering, unto the building up of the body of Christ."

The Bible, well-studied, fully believed, compassionately presented, and helpfully applied — is the answer to adult + world needs.

AIDS TO LEARNING

1. What is the significance of the long period of infancy of the human being? How alone can the infinite needs of humanity be supplied?

2. Why is the Bible supremely qualified to meet men's deepest needs? When is the Bible being used at its best?

3. Why is man's first and greatest need for a Saviour? How does the Bible help to meet this need?

4. What is a "motive"? What is the place of motives in human life? Make a list of a half-dozen motives that largely control adults today. Which of these need changing in order to be Christian?

5. Sum up in a few statements the incomparable value of the Bible in meeting present-day needs. How does this justify its designation as "the Book of books"?

6. What twofold lesson comes to the teacher of Sunday school adults as a result of this study? How may the teacher incorporate this discovery in his or her teaching?

Bible —
Book everybody buys & owns,
many believe in,
few love,
and hardly noone knows.

We must get people to know what the Bible says. S.S. was created for that purpose.

CHAPTER VI

THE ART OF BIBLE STUDY

OUTLINE

1. Why Adults Do Not "Study the Lesson"
2. Some Practical Rules of Study
3. An Illustration of Intelligent Lesson Study
4. The Fellowship of Bible Study
5. Using the Bible in the Class
6. The Joy of Fruitful Bible Knowledge

A popular writer once wrote a book about the Bible entitled, "The Book Nobody Knows." He took in too much territory, for there are many who know and love the Book. But if he had in mind the average adult Bible class he did not miss the fact very far. It is remarkable how little people know about the Bible who have attended Sunday school the better part of their lives. We dare not take for granted that men and women have an accurate understanding of the elementary facts of the Scriptures because they have lived in a land of churches and Sunday schools from their childhood.

Recently a simple Bible quiz was sent out to 18,344 high school students of a cultured Southern state. The returns revealed that 16,000 of them could not name three prophets in the Old Testament, that 12,000 could not name the four Gospels, and 10,000 could not give the names of three of Christ's disciples! One can be saved, and become an earnest and useful Christian, with very little knowledge of the Bible; but every Christian would be far richer and more fruitful if mind and heart were stored with knowledge of God's Word. Listening to another tell what he knows about the Bible has value, but far greater is the value that comes from personal study that results in the acquisition of truth for oneself. One of the next great steps forward in Sunday school progress is to bring a multitude of hungry-minded adults to know the joy of skill and achievement in the fine art of Bible study.

1. *Why Adults Do Not "Study the Lesson"*

"My class simply will not study the lesson," declares the typical teacher of adults, with an air of finality. Pressed to know why, the answers are unconvincing. "They are too busy," "They misplace their lesson helps," "They are too lazy," "They are not interested," "The Bible is too deep for them," "Not being in school, they have lost the study habit." Are these the real reasons? Digging deeper, we find three main reasons why many adults do not study the lesson:

First, *they do not know how to study*. The teacher urges the class to "study the lesson." Well, what shall one do? Read the Scripture passage indicated? Read the comment given in the lesson helps? Look up the questions in the *quarterly?* This is good as far as it goes, but presents too little challenge to interest and not enough reward for the effort expended. Experience proves that it is almost impossible to get average adults to keep up a scheme of study that requires a mechanical procedure of this sort.

What is "study?" It involves five main things: (1) a sufficient motive; (2) a problem to be solved; (3) materials and guidance for arriving at the solution; (4) a practical procedure; (5) use of the results. Suppose you wanted to learn to play the piano, or drive an automobile, or speak a foreign language. First, there would have to be a compelling reason for the undertaking. Next, you would face the difficulties involved. Then you would need materials of study—printed instructions, source materials, and so forth—and the help of a person

who has had experience. You would then want to know
what to do first, what to do next, and so on in orderly
progression. Last, but not least, it would be necesssary
for you to put into practice what you have learned.

These simple, common-sense requirements apply to
Bible study. We would not expect average adults to
study accounting or chemistry or designing or cookery or
nursing or the care and feeding of children or any other
of the scores of things that adults are constantly setting
themselves to learn if they had no motive, if they did
not appreciate the difficulty and value, if there were no
adequate sources of guidance and help, if practical steps
were not clearly outlined, if no use was made of the
things learned. When these elements are weak or missing, why should we expect busy adults to be Bible students? It is a proved fact that adults will study the
Bible when they understand what such study means and
are provided with the facilities for study.

Second, *adults have very little incentive to study*. A
wise teacher and leader once said that, after a lifetime
of study of human nature, he had reached this conclusion: we are all about as lazy as circumstances permit!
This may not be true of children and young people, but
it comes close to being one hundred per cent true of
adults. The pressure of demand on the time and energy
of most men and women is such that they rarely take
on extra duties unless there is some compelling incentive. They find time to do what they have to do and
what they want to do; but who can blame them for leaving off something that seems unnecessary? When a man
joins a typical adult Sunday school class he is often
impressed immediately with the fact that very few, even
of the old-timers, take lesson study seriously. He is
given some form of lesson help—a *quarterly*, a monthly
magazine, a lesson leaf—but he is not told what to do
with it. Rarely are advance assignments made. The
teacher seldom if ever refers to the lesson materials which
have been placed in the hands of the class. Since there
is no plan for study and since no directions are given

concerning the study, what is more natural than that the new member should fall in with the crowd and take it for granted that study is not expected? Thus the tradition is built up that a Sunday school is a school in name but not in fact, and that serious study, such as is required in any good day school, is out of order in the church school. Of course there are shining exceptions, and in an increasing number of Sunday schools study is done that would be a credit to any day school, but by and large adult classes have sadly lagged behind in this movement to put the teaching of the Bible on a sound educational basis.

How may this hurtful adult class tradition be broken up? Certainly not by quarreling with the class, nor by continually exhorting them to "study the lesson." The teacher must provide worthy incentives to study. One incentive is the recognition of lesson study by means of the Sunday School Record System. This system justly recognizes that the most important single point in the student's record is lesson study and gives the highest credit—thirty per cent—for attaining this point. A second incentive lies in the giving of definite directions for lesson study—the working out of interesting advance assignments—consisting of interesting questions to be looked up, parallel passages to be read, problems to be solved, projects to be carried out, application to actual situations to be made. A third indispensable type of incentive is the use of such study as members of the class may have done. It is unreasonable to expect people to give time and thought to study if the results are never called for or utilized by the teacher. Any teacher who will faithfully and enthusiastically bring to bear these three types of incentives on a class of intelligent adults will, in the course of a few months, secure a most gratifying response in lesson study.

2. *Some Practical Rules of Study*

Study, as we have seen, is more than reading what some one has written, or memorizing facts, or meditating

must think + solve problems

upon some one else's ideas. Study is thinking, and thinking is problem solving. There are certain conditions under which studying can be done to best advantage. If these conditions are absent, or if the rules are violated, study is made difficult and sometimes impossible. Here are some simple, practical rules of study that have been found helpful wherever tried:

(1) Keep yourself in good physical condition. *be active*

(2) Provide favorable conditions for study—proper light, temperature, chair, desk, and so forth. *no distraction*

(3) Have a regular time and place for study and form systematic habits of study. *early A.m—several times a wk.*

(4) Begin promptly, with an attitude of interest and attention. *Don't just read - actually study.*

(5) Determine the kind of study proposed—general reading, research, experimentation, logical reasoning, or a combination of these. *Know the Central idea —*

(6) Take a problem-solving attitude—seek for the difficulty involved, discover all possible pertinent facts, reason toward a conclusion, establish the conclusion. *read the whole Bible passage*

(7) As you read, underscore significant words and phrases; look up in your English dictionary and Bible dictionary words and allusions that you do not understand. Turn to parallel passages indicated by letters in the text that refer you to notes in the center and at the bottom of the page in your Bible. *look up marginal notes*

(8) Use your lesson helps not as a means of saving you from thinking but as means of helping you to discover the answers to your questions. Don't be afraid to raise questions—this is at the very heart of intelligent study.

(9) Make a careful written outline of the results of your study. *answer questions.*

(10) Find at once some practical use for what you have learned.

The rules suggested above are not given primarily for teachers, although the teacher will find them of value. The teacher's study will be dealt with in the next

Pupils should do these things.

(skip now to page 72.)

chapter. What is sought here is to give direction to the study of the class, to the end that every member of the class may become an intelligent and enthusiastic student of the Bible. A copy of these simple rules might well be pasted on the cover of the *quarterly,* and at the beginning of each quarter the rules might be reviewed and explained. What a change it would make if these rules were followed faithfully by the thousands of adult classes in our Sunday schools!

3. *An Illustration of Intelligent Lesson Study*

Let us picture a representative member of an adult Sunday school class who has decided to take the study of the Bible seriously, and who proposes to acquire a working mastery of the greatest of all books. How will he proceed?

First, *he will provide some quiet place suitable for study.* He will not waste energy trying to study in the midst of distractions—the blaring of the radio, the conversation of others, interruption and interference—if this can be avoided. On a convenient table will be Bible, lesson helps, books, paper and pencil.

Second, *he will have a regular time set apart for study.* The best time is early morning when everything is quiet and the mind is fresh. Ten minutes to a half-hour before breakfast every day is ideal. As a rule, much better results are obtained from briefer periods of daily study than from one long period. If this is not practicable, time may be found on certain evenings, say Monday, Wednesday and Friday. Saturday night, Sunday morning and Sunday afternoon may prove to be the most available time, though there are disadvantages in waiting so late to study the immediate lesson, and having so long an interval between the study and the class discussion of the next lesson. The main point, however, is to have a regular schedule and stick to it.

Third, *our intelligent Bible student will devise a plan of study.* He will not confuse study with casual reading.

A certain amount of general reading enters into study, but must not constitute the whole of it. The intelligent student approaches his study with enthusiasm and purpose, and follows a plan that leads to definite results. The plan will vary with individuals, and there will be variety for the sake of interest with a given person, but as we watch a successful student we find him following a procedure something like this:

(1) The location of the Bible materials to be studied by reference to the *quarterly* or other lesson help—not just the brief printed passage, but the lesson as a whole.

(2) The reading of the Bible passages, thoughtfully and prayerfully, to get a first impression of their total message. This should be done before reading the comments in the *quarterly*.

(3) The raising of certain basic questions: What is the central idea of the larger lesson, around which everything else seems to revolve? What main problem does this raise? What do I want to get from this study? What practical use can I make of it right now and in the future?

(4) The raising of more detailed questions, as to date, place, authorship, context, the writer's purpose, connection with previous lessons in the series, meaning of unfamiliar words and phrases, significance of strange allusions and unusual ideas.

(5) The use of lesson helps to answer the questions which have thus arisen—the Bible itself first of all, looking up marginal notes and cross references, and turning to maps, dictionary, concordance; and then the comments of the lesson writer in the *quarterly*.

(6) The underscoring of words, phrases, verses, in order to make them stand out clearly, that bear out the main thought of the lesson; or that need further study for clearing up of their meaning.

(7) The construction of a written outline of the results which may well be in answer to the questions:

What does this lesson say? What does it mean? What does it teach? How is it to be put into practice?

Does such a procedure seem to expect too much? Not if we are in earnest when we say that the Bible is the greatest of all books, and its teachings the most precious of all truths. Is there not grave inconsistency in exalting the Bible as we do, and then cheapening it by assuming that intelligent men and women will not take a program of systematic study seriously? The adults of our Bible classes can be led, by the thousands, to such a program of study, and the next step in Sunday school progress is a mighty movement to make this vision a reality!

This is why we have S S

4. *The Fellowship of Bible Study*

Study alone is at best a rather lonesome business. This is why students find it much more difficult to get the same results from a correspondence course as from school attendance. When two or more people study together there is the stimulus of mind reacting to mind, and the contagion of interest and enthusiasm. It is not impossible for an isolated individual to study the Bible, but it is improbable. If we would maintain our zeal for Bible study, we must become members of a community of Bible students. This is one of the principal reasons why we should diligently seek to enrol every possible adult in a Sunday school class—it enormously increases the possibility of his becoming a student of the Bible.

In an enthusiastic class of Bible students, the arithmetic of the Scriptures is demonstrated—"and five of you shall chase a hundred, and a hundred of you shall chase ten thousand: and your enemy shall fall before you by the sword." Five adults banded together in a church can vanquish a hundred enemies of indifference, ignorance, doubt, temptation; but a hundred such adults banded together for Bible study, can, with the sword of the Spirit, put to flight ten thousand such enemies. Here are three tested rules for maintaining Bible study at a high level:

1. We can learn the Bible alone — but won't.

2. Being interested in getting others to learn gives us incentive to learn & love God's Word

(1) *Enlist others in Bible study.* When we become interested deeply in a movement or in a cause we immediately seek to bring others to its support. This is true in politics, in business, in education, in social and civic enterprises, in charitable and benevolent undertakings. The principle holds equally good in the enlistment of men and women in the study of the Bible. Once we discover the Bible, and its power becomes to us real and precious and transforming, it is both natural and necessary that we try to bring others to a similar experience. When we are gripped by this purpose we go afield with compelling persuasion to bring others into the circle of students of God's Word. It is with this argument for joining a Sunday school that "we compel them to come in."

3. Study yourself—Know something—then share

(2) *Share with others the fruits of your Bible study.* When we make a great discovery of any kind we at once want to share it with those we love. Should you find a medicine that cured you of a dreaded disease, nothing could keep you from sharing this secret with a loved one suffering from the same disease. When through the Bible you find life in Christ, the forgiveness of sin, peace that passeth understanding, the solution to your most difficult problems and the satisfaction to your deepest needs, can you remain content until you find others who are in the dark and share with them your light? The love of Christ in the heart brings the love of all men everywhere, so that you yearn to share with everybody the Book that you have found infinitely precious. With a passion like this in our hearts, we go out not just to invite people to attend Sunday school, but to give them a taste of the joy which we have found through the Bible and to implant in them the desire for the same rich fruit.

the Christian shares!

(3) *Join with others in the quest for more truth.* Our study of the Bible should not end with our Sunday school study. The Sunday school lessons open the door to a vast treasure house of spiritual riches. One of the sur-

4. Set an attitude of yearning for Bible knowledge in your life & in others

prises of Bible study is that the more we know the more we discover there is to know. To the student of the Bible there comes an ever increasing desire for more knowledge and understanding. Beyond the Sunday school class lie many opportunities for further study. The richest of these opportunities is the preaching service. The minister is a specialist in Bible study and from the Scriptures, like the householder in the parable, he brings forth treasures new and old. What a joy it is to the preacher to have before him a congregation of eager Bible students who are joining with him in the quest for more truth! The mid-week prayer service affords another splendid opportunity for fellowship in Bible study. In the prayer meeting an ideal situation is provided not only for learning more about the Bible in a spiritually minded and congenial group, but for giving expression to what has already been learned. The programs in the Adult Union are based on the Bible and active participation in this organization will bring further happy fellowship in Bible study. For the women the Missionary Society, and for the men the Brotherhood, enlarge still further the field of study of the Bible with others.

Some of life's greatest values come as by-products of such fellowship in Bible study. Acquaintances are made, friendships are formed, opportunities for service are opened up, and souls are won to Christ when men and women join together in earnest and enthusiastic Bible study. Why not lay hold on this conception of a Sunday school class, and beyond it the church in all its activities and organizations, as being essentially a fellowship of Bible students, learning the will of God through his Word and then putting what has been learned into practice?

5. *Using the Bible in the Class*

The meeting of the class on Sunday should be thought of as the climax to a week of Bible study. The Bibles that have been read and marked during the week should be in the hands of their owners unfailingly on Sunday during the class period. With open Bibles and open minds, the class should then bring together the results of their study, their unanswered questions, their unsolved problems, their new light and fresh experience, their suggestions for practical application. Sometimes teachers complain that adults will not bring their Bibles to the class. Of course they will not if they are never used. Consider these practical and suggestive ways in which the Bible may be used during the class hour:

(1) Let the key passage or passages constituting the heart of the lesson be read by members of the class. Give variety to this reading—all reading in concert, or reading alternatively, or reading responsively, or a selected group standing and reading together, or reading dramatically.

(2) Let questions be raised and the answers given by reference to appropriate verses from the Scriptures. Much useless debate and wasted time in discussion would be avoided if the Bible itself were taken as the court of appeal and its answers accepted as final.

(3) Let attention be directed to the meaning of certain key verses. Time will not suffice for emphasis on everything in any lesson. It is usually wise to concentrate on one or two great truths found in key verses.

(4) Let difficult or disputed meanings be interpreted by reference to related passages found elsewhere. It is a truism that the Bible is its own best interpreter.

(5) Let various members of the class point out truths which they have found especially enlightening and helpful. These truths can then be fitted into the teacher's lesson outline.

(6) Let reports be made, based on previous assignments, by designated members of the class. One member may report on what he has been able to learn about the geography of the lesson, another on the historical setting, another on the principal characters, another on

difficult passages, another on debatable meanings, another on related teachings, another on practical applications.

(7) Let an interesting project be undertaken—the making of a series of illustrated maps, or the preparation of notebooks, or the carrying out of a historical investigation, or the rendering of a practical service. Such a project, to be successful, must grow out of the interest of the class itself and be vitally related to the Bible study in hand.

Can adults be induced to bring their Bibles to the class? Certainly they can, if regular and intelligent use of the Bible is made during the class hour. There are many things an adult Bible class may not do, but perhaps the most inexcusable of its omissions is the failure to use open Bibles during the class period. How can we ever hope to get people started on a course of serious Bible study if in the classroom there are no Bibles present, and in the teaching of the lesson Bibles are not used?

6. *The Joy of Fruitful Bible Knowledge*

The lives of many adult Christians are strangely devoid of the note of joy. There is no song in their hearts nor on their lips. They go to Sunday school and church, and perform some of the routine duties of giving and serving, but there is no note of enthusiasm about it. They have accepted Christ as Saviour and have obeyed him in baptism and church membership, but he often seems to them to be afar off, and his love is an abstraction rather than a personal reality. Sometimes they become gravely backslidden, compromising with the world and falling into known sin. What is the matter with these half-hearted, defeated Christians?

The Psalmist said, "Thy Word have I hid in my heart, that I might not sin against thee." The Bible keeps from sin and sin keeps from the Bible. One may be a Christian, saved by God's grace through Christ, and yet be a weak and fruitless Christian. Let such a Christian become a real student of the Bible, let him saturate his mind and heart in its truths, let him join with others

1. People need joy.
2. Will get real joy from knowing God's Word
3. "   "   "   peace   "   "   answers to life's problems.

in its study and practice, and new life will come as when refreshing rain soaks the roots of the grass after a drouth. Would you know the joy of the Lord? Then let the Lord speak to you out of his Book, and your lost joy will be restored!

There are many forms of useful and fruitful knowledge. Can any knowledge be compared in value with that of the Bible? A man may have all the learning of the schools and yet be essentially ignorant if he does not know the Bible. A man may never have been inside the walls of a school, and yet be truly educated if he knows God's Word. So long as Bibles are plentiful, and Bible classes with open arms welcome men and women to its study, there is no excuse for any man or woman complaining that they have been denied the privileges of education.

Supremely important is the joy and peace that the Bible brings to those who are without God and without hope in its revelation of the gospel as the power of God unto salvation to every one that believes. How can the lost sinner know the love of God in Christ, as told in a thousand ways in the Bible, and yet reject that love? Isaiah's word is as true today as when he wrote it: "For as the rain cometh down and the snow from heaven, and returneth not thither, but watereth the earth and maketh it bring forth and bud, and giveth seed to the sower and bread to the eater; so shall my word be that goeth forth out of my mouth; it shall not return unto me void, but it shall accomplish that which I please, and it shall prosper in the thing whereto I sent it."

The Adult Bible Class movement has had several stages of development in which the emphasis has been placed on numbers, organization, activities, lecturing, discussion, fellowship, social service, and the like. Why not frankly put all these things in the circumference, and Bible study at the center? Other agencies will do other things—if the Sunday school class does not lead men and women to know and love the Bible it will not be done. Does this narrow the circle of the class' interests and influence? By no means! Out of a true revival of Bible study on the part of the adults of our churches will flow all else for which spiritual Christianity stands. Shall we not give ourselves with renewed prayer and devotion to the promotion of a worldwide movement of enthusiastic Bible study as the basis of a genuine and desperately needed revival of religion?

AIDS TO LEARNING

1. What are some inadequate reasons as to why adults generally do not study the Sunday school lesson? Give two principal reasons why they do not study the Bible.

2. What do you do when you "study"? Indicate five things that are essential to real study. Illustrate from some study other than of the Bible. Show that these requirements apply no less to Bible study.

3. How would you now define "study"? Select and re-state in your own words at least six of the "Rules of Study" given in the chapter.

4. In the light of the study of procedures and rules indicated, take next Sunday's lesson and show, step by step, how it should be studied for best results.

5. How could this plan of study be presented to an average class of Sunday school adults so as to secure its adoption and use?

6. Why insist that adults bring their Bibles to the class? State briefly a half-dozen practical ways in which Bibles may be used during the class period.

No one can effectively do anything consistently without preparation of heart, conscience, life, & intellect

CHAPTER VII

THE TEACHER PREPARING TO TEACH

OUTLINE

1. Consider Those to Be Taught
2. Master the Lesson Materials
3. Connect Bible Truths with Class Needs
4. Plan to Secure Class Response
5. Determine Aims and How to Reach Them
6. Construct an Effective Teaching Outline
7. Tools for the Teacher's Use

Teaching is both an art and a science. As an art it requires insight, grasp, spiritual sensitiveness, concentration, devotion. As a science it demands unceasing effort, determination, accuracy, enthusiasm, specialized ability. No artist ever achieved true success who did not pay the price of preparation. No scientist ever made good in his work who did not fit himself by long training for the task. Need it be argued that the only guarantee for success on the part of the teacher, who must be both an artist and a scientist, is adequate preparation?

Next Sunday you are to stand before a class of adults as their teacher. Do you not tremble at the responsibility? Of course your first and greatest need is preparation of yourself. Your heart must be right with God, your relation to Christ must be warm and vital, your sense of the presence of the Holy Spirit must be real, your fellowship with your fellowman must be unbroken. If there is anything that separates between you and God, or between you and another, get it out of the way before you go further!

[79]

Get off to yourself — get proper equipment (books)

Taking it for granted that your heart is right, and that you are genuinely interested in your work, what next? You must have a regular time for study, certainly not less than two hours a week. You should have a quiet, comfortable place for study, where there will be a minimum of distractions. You should have practical facilities for study—a work desk or table, a good teacher's Bible with helps, an English dictionary and a Bible dictionary, as many good commentaries as you can afford, *The Sunday School Builder, Sunday School Adults* or other lesson helps used by the class, the *Teacher* and similar teacher's helps, and your class roll with records kept up to date. Pencil and paper, and possibly a typewriter, will complete the essential equipment.

Seated at your table, conscious of your responsibility for teaching your class next Sunday, what are the steps in a sensible procedure of lesson preparation?

1. *Consider Those to Be Taught*

The first step in the teacher's specific preparation should be a careful look at the class roll-book or the class record cards. It is of fundamental importance for the teacher to realize at the very beginning that he is not primarily to teach *a lesson* but *a class*. He is to teach people by means of Bible truth, and the plan of teaching will necessarily be largely determined by the nature and needs of those to be taught.

As the teacher studies the class roll he will note a good many things. Who have been regular and irregular in attendance? Who are on time and who are usually tardy? Who bring their Bibles? What is revealed by the offering or lack of it? Who report a prepared lesson? Who attend the preaching service faithfully? A careful study of the facts thus revealed will bring to the teacher a keen realization of the human element involved in the class make-up.

Know your class members. What are their needs? Who will bother? — Will they study lessons? bring Bibles?

Taking in turn each name represented, the teacher will undertake to visualize the person. What do you know about each one of these people? Who are Christians and who are not? Who are faithful and loyal and who are careless and indifferent? What background of Bible knowledge can be assumed? Who can be safely called on without risking embarrassment? Who must be watched to see that he does not do all the talking and answer all the questions? What problems and difficulties are some facing? What spiritual struggles are some passing through?

As the teacher passes such questions as these through his mind, he will be constrained to pause frequently for prayer. May the Holy Spirit help us to lead this unsaved soul to Christ! May God give grace to this dear man or woman who is passing through the deep waters! May Christ tighten his grip on this one whom Satan is sifting! May wisdom from above be given to this father and mother whose hearts are being broken by a wayward child! God grant health and strength to this one who has been ill! May the love of Christ break down the barriers that have separated these friends! As the teacher thus prays he will often be moved to go to see this one or that one or the other one, or to call up some member of the class and request that the visit be made. Then, as he settles himself to the work of lesson preparation, the teacher will feel the warm glow of human interest and the moving of the Holy Spirit on his mind to discover in the lesson just those truths that will best meet these deep human needs.

2. *Master the Lesson Materials*

Turning to the lesson guide, the teacher will note the passage or passages that have been selected by the lesson committee for special study. He will turn back to refresh his memory concerning the previous lessons in the series, and then he will look ahead to see what lesson immediately follows. Now he will begin in the Bible

1. Refresh on last lesson + quarterly Emphasis
2. Look forward to where next lessons are going
3. Read total Bible Material
4. Clear up background materials + questions

where the last lesson left off, and read carefully but rapidly to where the present lesson ends. This reading will be done in order to get the whole context in mind, and not for detailed analysis.

With the larger lesson thus clearly in view the teacher's next step is to clear up what is not fully understood. This will probably involve questions concerning date and authorship, purpose and problems, unfamiliar words and expressions, unusual ideas and allusions. Carefully and methodically the teacher must use available helps until these questions have been answered and his thinking is definite and clear. Preparation at this point is not complete until the teacher has such familiarity with the lesson materials that he feels reasonably competent to answer any questions which may arise growing out of the lesson text and its study.

3. Connect Bible Truths with Class Needs

The teacher's mastery of the lesson materials is not to the end that he may tell the class what he knows about these facts, however interesting they may be. Two things should now stand side by side in consciousness—the truths of the lesson, and the needs of the class. It is the teacher's task to make the connection. The question now is: What issue, or difficulty, or problem emerges from the lesson as a whole that has definite relationship to the interests and needs of the class? Often the lesson title for adults will give a valuable clue. This, however, must not be followed slavishly, for sometimes the title is rather strained and farfetched, and sometimes it may suggest a line of thought that is removed from the real need of the class.

The teacher cannot depend on some one else to determine for him what he shall make the center of the lesson, about which other ideas shall be made to gather. He must be careful not to let his own interest and need decide the question. With consecrated imagination, he must try to project himself into the lives of members of his class as he seeks to determine what will constitute for them a real life problem which will command their attention because it presents a felt difficulty. It will, of course, not be possible to deal with every need of every member of the class in every lesson. The teacher will concentrate at one time upon bringing the lost to a decision, at another time upon comforting those who are in sorrow, at still another time upon strengthening those who are undergoing temptation, and again upon enlisting the indifferent in active service. But always there should be the sense of meeting some definite need or needs, and the selection of major truths for emphasis with a view to achieving this definite end.

4. *Plan to Secure Class Response*

We know this to be true—learning is the outcome of responding. The response which the teacher seeks is threefold—thinking, feeling, and willing. How can the members of the class be stimulated to think? How can their emotions be aroused? How can they be led to make decisions and carry them out into action? These questions bring the teacher to the very heart of his problem of preparation. It is difficult to know in advance just how to secure such responses. The teacher cannot predict exactly what the situation will be, what questions will be asked, what incidents may arise. But within limits he can plan to devise situations to which the class will react in somewhat predictable fashion.

For instance, the teacher may plan to ask questions that will certainly provoke thought and discussion. Such questions are not merely for the purpose of fact-finding, but probe into the deep things of life. The teacher should devise carefully in advance these thought questions, and introduce them skilfully at the points where they will evoke thought and discussion. Then, the teacher may plan to arouse feeling by presenting sharply contrasting views, out of which will emerge issues that stir the heart. Personal testimony and experience, illustrations taken from life, situations that move to laughter or tears may be planned by the teacher to the end that the class be made to feel deeply as well as to think clearly. Then, the teacher must never overlook the fact that the moving of the will is the ultimate purpose of his teaching. The teacher's planning is incomplete until he clearly visualizes what he wants to take place in new decisions, higher planes of living, and changed attitudes and habits.

It is obvious that such responses as are here indicated will not be secured if the teacher does all the talking. True, there may be inward responses, that give no vocal expression; but these silent responses tend to be feeble and impermanent. The chances that responses will become fixed, that is, that learnings will take place, are greatly enhanced when they are given expression in words and deeds. The teacher should ask himself in advance: Who is going to do most of the talking in the teaching of this lesson? Who will ask and answer most of the questions? What opportunity am I giving to the class to participate in the lesson period? If the teacher does practically all of the responding, it follows that the teacher will do most of the learning. The teacher may enjoy this, but is it fair to the class? Let the teacher know assuredly that he will do a relatively poor piece of teaching, if, in his planning, he has not definitely made a place for the securing of responses on the part of the class.

5. *Determine Aims and How to Reach Them*

"One reason some folks don't git nowhar," Hambone once remarked, "is because they warn't gwine nowhar when dey started." All through this process of preparation the teacher should constantly have been asking, "What are my aims?" It is not enough just to aim to teach an interesting lesson. It is not enough just to desire to do good through the teaching of the Bible. It is not enough just to hope that desirable results will follow if the class listens with reasonable interest to a talk, or lecture, or discussion based on the Bible. The teacher's general aims may be entirely commendable, and yet the specific aims for a given lesson may be weak and vague. How may the teacher determine concrete aims that should be steadily kept in mind in every step of the procedure in the preparation of the lesson?

An aim, to be valuable, must begin where people are in a world as it is. High-sounding, theoretical, abstract aims are of little value in this work-a-day world. A good aim is one that constantly moves from lower to higher, thus giving direction to thought and activity. A worthy aim will set people thinking for themselves, so that the aim will become their own and not merely be imposed upon them. An aim that will stand the test must be in line with the purposes of Jesus as revealed in the New Testament.

Have you ever tried to make a list of simple, practical, aims that you would like to see achieved through your teaching in the lives of members of your class? Examine this list of fundamental abilities which every teacher ought to aim to develop in those whom he teaches: (1) to use, understand, and love the Bible; (2) to participate in discussion; (3) to engage in worship; (4) to co-operate in activities; (5) to give intelligently; (6) to serve efficiently; (7) to be a good church member; (8) to be a happy member of a Christian family; (9) to be an honest, useful, upright citizen; (10) to love Christ and seek to win others to him and to his service. This list is by no means exhaustive, but illustrates the point concerning the need for simple, concrete objectives which should always be kept before the teacher as he plans to teach. The teacher should make his own list of aims and this list he should review again and again. At every point in his lesson preparation, the question should be asked, To what extent will this lesson, as I propose to teach it, contribute to the attainment of these definite ends?

6. *Construct an Effective Teaching Outline*

It is imperative that the teacher reduce the results of his lesson preparation to writing. It may not be necessary or even desirable to take the written notes to the classroom, but failure to put on paper the results of one's study is nearly always wasteful and inefficient. The filing away, week by week, of teaching outlines gives one a rich storehouse from which to draw as the years come and go. Even more important are the habits of accuracy and thoroughness that are built up by such a practice. While of course no teacher should be a slave to a written outline, the possession of a carefully constructed lesson plan, easily referred to during the teaching period, is one of the best preventives of side-tracking and incompleteness in teaching.

There is a distinct difference between the outline of the lesson passage and a teaching outline. The outline of the lesson is a logical arrangement, under heads and sub-heads, of the facts or truths contained in the Scripture portion. Such an analysis of the teaching materials is indispensable, and has its place in the teaching plan. The teaching outline is a blue-print of the procedure which the teacher has planned to use, from beginning to conclusion. An effective teaching outline would certainly include:

(1) How to create a favorable atmosphere in which to teach.

(2) How to get the Bible passage or passages attractively read.

(3) How to get a good start that will compel attention and sustain interest.

(4) How to shift from the attention-compelling beginning to the heart of the lesson.

(5) How to concentrate the thought of the class on the significant life-problem that connects the Bible truth with class needs.

(6) How to make known that which is unknown and clear up that which is misunderstood.

(7) How to secure a maximum of class participation.

(8) How to guide the procedures from point to point so as to arrive at a satisfactory conclusion within the time limits.

(9) How to direct what has been learned into practical channels.

(10) How to secure definite study of the next lesson.

This, it can be readily seen, is far different from preparing the outline of a speech based on the lesson. It recognizes that teaching is not telling, nor provoking random discussion, nor hearing a recitation, but rather the stimulation and guidance of experience, growing out of life interests and needs, with the divinely inspired Scriptures as the source of wisdom and authority. Teaching thus conceived makes the Bible a living reality. The teacher who thus prepares to teach is literally obeying the exhortation of Paul: "Give diligence to present thyself approved unto God, a workman that needeth not to be ashamed, handling aright the word of truth."

7. *Tools for the Teacher's Use*

An elaborate chest of tools does not guarantee a good workman; but the best workman is almost helpless without a few good tools. Given a saw, a hammer, a plane, a pair of pliers, a screw-driver, a wrench, a footrule, a good carpenter can manage to do good work; but provide him with a full chest of well-chosen tools, and he will do far better work. The Sunday school teacher should provide the absolutely necessary teaching accessories at once, and then go forward in the gradual accumulation of a workshop that will enable him to be indeed "a workman that needeth not to be ashamed."

8. *Equipment for Classroom and Desk*

(1) Complete set of Sunday School Record System supplies for class secretary.

(2) Folders describing department and class organization and giving duties of officers.

(3) A good blackboard for the teacher's use.

(4) Improved class blackboard, arranged for reporting the class by groups.

(5) Department and Class Standard charts.

(6) Copies of one or more of the following lesson helps distributed regularly to members of the class: *Sunday School Adults; Points for Emphasis; On the Wing with the Word*.

(7) One or more of the following helps for the teacher: *The Teacher; The Sunday School Builder; Peloubet's Notes; Tarbell's Teacher's Guide*, or *Broadman Comments* (bound volumes).

(8) A Six-Point Teacher's Individual Record Book, with complete information concerning each member of the class, Sunday by Sunday.

(9) A loose-leaf notebook, with a page or more for each member enrolled, on which the teacher will, from time to time, make notes of what he has learned about the individual's religious condition, needs, capacities, special abilities, problems, difficulties, progress, and so forth.

(10) A quiet place at home or elsewhere set apart as a sanctuary for study and prayer, and a regular schedule for work and worship.

9. *General Helps for Bible Study*

(1) A Teacher's Bible (this includes maps, references, brief dictionary, concordance, and so forth).

(2) A Bible Dictionary (Hastings, or Smith, or Davis, one volume).

(3) A Dictionary of the English Language.

(4) A Bible Concordance (Crudens or Young or Strong).

(5) A Topical Bible (Naves or System Bible).

(6) A reliable commentary or set of commentaries: one volume—Dummelow or Jamieson, Fausset and Brown; set—American; Expositors; Maclaren's; Carroll; or The Expositor's Bible.

(7) A Standard Encyclopedia (*International, Britannica, Americana*).

(8) *Harmony of the Gospels,* Broadus and Robertson.

(9) *Bible Atlas,* Hurlbut.

10. *Books in Sunday School Board's Training Course Leading to Blue and Gold Seal Diploma:*

Four fundamental books lead to the Diploma. The full course comprises seven groups which lead progressively to the highest award. Four books after the Diploma lead to the Red Seal; four more books lead to the Blue Seal; four more books lead to the Gold Seal. The texts change from time to time. The approved current list may be had at any time from the Sunday School Department of the Baptist Sunday School Board.

11. *Books on the Bible for the Teacher's Library*

The Heart of the Old Testament, by John R. Sampey.

The Twelve Minor Prophets, by Geo. L. Robinson.

The Dramatic Story of the Old Testament, by Ira M. Price.

Historical Geography of the Holy Land; Isaiah; the Twelve Prophets, by George Adam Smith.

The Doctrines of the Prophets, by A. F. Kirkpatrick.

Great Men and Women of the Bible, 6 volumes, by James Hastings.

Life and Times of the Patriarchs, by W. H. Thomson.

Heroes of Israel, by W. G. Blaikie.

Life and Works of Christ, by John Cunningham Geikie.

Life and Times of Jesus the Messiah, by Edersheim, 2 Vols.

Epochs in the Life of Jesus; Epochs in the Life of Paul; John the Loyal; Word Pictures in the New Testament, by A. T. Robertson.

Parables of the Kingdom, by G. Campbell Morgan.

Parables of Our Saviour; Miracles of Our Saviour, by William Taylor.

Life of Christ; Life of Paul, by James Stalker.

Biblical Backgrounds, by J. McKee Adams.

The Life and Letters of Saint Paul, by David Smith.

The Days of His Flesh, by David Smith.

How the New Testament Came to Be Written, by W. O. Carver.

Notes on the Miracles of Our Lord, by Richard C. Trench.

Christian Doctrines, by W. T. Conner.

The Christian Religion in Its Doctrinal Expression, by E. Y. Mullins.

12. *Books on Teaching and Adult Interests*

Adults in the Sunday School, by Willliam P. Phillips.

Adults and The Art of Learning, by M. J. Andrews.

Creative Teaching, by J. W. Suter.

How to Teach in the Church School, by Paul H. Vieth.

You Can Learn to Teach, by Margaret Slattery.

Teaching Religion, by A. J. W. Myers.

Improving Your Teaching, by Frank M. McKibben.

The Art of Jesus as a Teacher, by C. F. McKoy.

Education for Life with God, by Wilfred E. Powell.

Toward an Understanding of Adults, by Earl F. Ziegler.

Young Adults and the Church, by Jessie A. Charters.

Adult Interests, and Adult Learning, by Edward L. Thorndike.

The Church and Adult Education, by B. F. Winchester.

Adult Education, by J. K. Hart.

The Meaning of Adult Education, by Edouard C. Lindeman.

Why Stop Learning?, by Dorothy Canfield Fisher.

Guiding Individual Growth, by Roy A. Burkhart.

Life Begins at Forty, by W. B. Pitkin.

The Arts of Leisure, by Barstow Greenbie.

Character Education, by Harry C. McKown.

Growth in Religion, by Harold J. Sheridan.

Growth in Christian Personality, by Wilfred E. Powell.

Sweeping the Cobwebs, by L. J. Martin and Clare de Gruchy.

CHAPTER VIII

THE ADULT TEACHER IN ACTION

OUTLINE

1. Creating a Favorable Atmosphere
2. Getting a Good Start
3. Stimulating Thought and Discussion
4. Guiding and Controlling the Procedure
5. Arriving at Conclusions
6. Putting Truth Into Action

It is Sunday morning. The people have gathered in the house of God on his day to study his Book. In a few minutes you are to stand before your class to lead them in the study of the lesson. Let us assume that you have made reasonably adequate preparation both of heart and of mind. Let us hope that you are physically fit, mentally alert, and spiritually alive. Before you are hungry-hearted men or women whose minds crave truth from the Bible about God and life. In your hand is the Book. Your watch indicates that you have about thirty golden minutes in which to put into action what you have been planning all the week. Many things are important—records, reports, organization, visitation, service activities—but these fade into the background as you rise and stand before the class to teach. What are you going to do and how are you going to do it?

1. *Creating a Favorable Atmosphere*

It would be interesting to know what the members of a typical adult class are thinking about as they enter the church building. It would be safe to guess that not many

[93]

1. Adult's thoughts on Sun. A.M. will not be on lesson
2. Opening Assem. cannot create right atmosphere
3. But use the spirit created by opening Assem.

of them are thinking about the lesson. If consciousness were represented by a series of concentric circles, certain personal interests would, for the majority, be found at the center, while the Bible lesson would be distinctly in the outer fringe—if present at all. The first problem of the teacher is to reverse this situation—getting other things in the fringe of consciousness, and the truths to be taught in the center.

How may this be done? Not suddenly, but gradually, to be most effective. Herein lies the value of the adult department program. Instead of miscellaneous "opening exercises"—which, as some one has remarked, neither open anything nor exercise anybody—a brief program should be carefully devised that creates an atmosphere of reverence, engages all in singing, prayer, reading, and focuses attention on the primary object for which all are present—the study of the Bible lesson. If, in a small school, the department program is impossible, the same principle should apply in planning and carrying out the opening program of the general assembly.

When the class assembles care should be taken not to dissipate the values which have come from the joint meeting just described. Every effort should be made to reduce distractions to a minimum. Class business, reports of officers, the taking of the records should be dispatched quickly and quietly. A lengthy class program of special music, talks and reports, introduction of visitors and new members, entertainment features, election of officers, back-slapping and hand-clapping, is wholly out of order and defeats the main purpose for which the class exists. Class business and social features should be given the right-of-way in the monthly week-day meeting of the class. The Sunday session should be characterized by the hush of reverence and the turning of every soul to God for new light and life from his Book.

The necessary affairs of the class having been attended to, quickly and orderly, the key passage or passages constituting the Bible lesson should then be attractively read.

A moment of prayer, as all heads are bowed, and then the teacher steps forward to teach, in an atmosphere of reverent expectancy.

2. *Getting a Good Start*

The first three minutes are crucial. In them the teacher may get off to a good start or a poor start. If he hesitates, makes some trite remark, apologizes or otherwise calls attention to himself, or makes statements that are abstract and uninteresting, the chances are very great that the lesson period will be a relative failure. If, on the other hand, the teacher begins with confidence and self-forgetfulness, compels attention and excites interest and the desire for reponse, the battle is half won.

The first essential of teaching is the securing of attention. Attention is the power of the mind to select one stimulus out of many and hold it, at least momentarily, in the focus of consciousness. This can be done by force of will, but forced attention involves strain that soon becomes painful. The most satisfactory type of attention is free, involuntary, unstrained. Such attention arises spontaneously when something striking and unusual occurs, or when a familiar truth is presented in a new way, or when a problem involving a personal felt difficulty is confronted. Attention refuses to respond when the stimulus is either beyond the range of what is already known, or is trite and familiar.

Attention therefore depends upon two conditions—there must be the element of the unknown combined with the element of the known. This principle is exemplified when the teacher begins by making a striking statement based on everyday experience; or tells a story that illustrates the truth to be taught; or asks a question or sets up a problem related to the lesson but growing out of human experience. However he may secure it, let the teacher be assured of this: There will be no teaching and no learning without attention.

Attention, at best, is flitting. It is like a butterfly that dips from flower to flower. Only a trained student can maintain attention concentrated on a single thought for more than a few seconds. *Attention, therefore, must be deepened into interest.* Interest is the power of the mind to keep a connected series of ideas in the center of consciousness over a period of time. The teacher's next problem is to deepen attention into sustained interest.

Interest demands that there be a bond or connection between the idea and the person to whom it is presented. Unconsciously, when a teacher begins to make statements, the hearers are saying to themselves, "Well, what of it? What has that to do with me? What difference does it make in my life?" If there appears to be no connection, but the ideas are abstract and remote, the listener almost certainly "loses interest"—that is he fails to make and sustain the connection. This does not mean that the appeal must be made to self-interest, for many of our deepest concerns lie outside ourselves; but it does mean that a tie must be established that binds the thought of the teacher to the experience of the learner.

A good start in teaching is made, accordingly, when the teacher begins on the plane of familiar human experience and goes by natural stages to that which is less familiar or unknown. Instead of beginning with explanations as to date, authorship, historical setting, events, obscure meanings, doctrines, and the like, the teacher will follow the example of Jesus and begin with human interest situations and problems. From these, like Jesus, he will then proceed to what is not known or understood. The teacher will not always find it easy to practice this principle, but he may rest absolutely assured of this truth: Where there is no sustained interest there will be no teaching or learning.

3. *Stimulating Thought and Discussion*

Having got off to a good start, what is the teacher's next function? If telling were teaching he could proceed for the next twenty-five minutes to deliver a talk or lecture, in which he would re-state, under appropriate headings, the content of the lesson, clarifying and illustrating its meaning, and closing with a practical application. The fact remains, however, that telling is *not* teaching. A certain amount of telling enters into teaching as instruction, but teaching must go farther than the conveying to the pupil of what the teacher has learned. We instantly recognize this to be true when we consider the teaching and learning of a practical skill. No one ever learned to swim, or to skate, or to drive an automobile, or to cook, or to play the piano, by listening to some one lecture on the subject. Nor can one learn to write good English, or do arithmetic, or draw maps, or speak a foreign language, or anything else worthwhile, who has listened to another talk about it but has had no personal experience.

There is no teaching without learning, and no learning without responding. The response may be one of thought, of emotion, of will, made silently, or it may be given expression in words or deeds. Learning takes place best when there is a mental response accompanied by a physical expression.

The teacher's business is to create a situation in which the members of the class will be challenged to think, and then led to ask and answer questions, to seek authoritative information, and to call upon their own and others' experiences. Here is a lesson from the first chapter of John's Gospel. The teacher may have gripped attention by picturing the aged Apostle as he begins to write, moved by the Holy Spirit. His mind goes back over the history-making years since Pentecost, back to the ascension, the resurrection, the crucifixion; back to those glorious years when he and the other disciples companied with Jesus in the flesh; back to the thirty years of obscurity in Nazareth, then back to the holy birth at Bethlehem. Can he go back further than this? Yes! With inspired vision John goes back into the councils of eternity, before the Word, which was God, became flesh and dwelt among men. Surely attention will have deepened into interest as this unique introduction is given to the familiar story of the birth of Jesus.

Now it is time to challenge thought. Why does John refer to Jesus Christ, before his birth, as the Word? What is a word? What is the purpose of words? Since words are the means by which man communicates with man, is it not fitting that Jesus Christ should be called the Word of God, seeing that he is God's revelation of himself to man? By now many questions will be arising in the minds of the class. The teacher will continue to raise further questions. Not speculation, but authoritative answers are needed. Where get them? From the Bible itself, of course. Following a careful outline of Scripture material, the teacher's part is to make one question lead to another, one answer suggest the next. He is happiest when the class has forgotten that they are in a classroom and he is the formal teacher, and all are joining in the search for truth. The more questions are asked and the more individuals take part, the better he is pleased with the situation. He knows that real teaching is going on, and that the members of his class are learning something, as he abandons the role of lecturer or drill-master and becomes an effective stimulator of thought and discussion. To the members of the class comes the deep satisfaction of realizing that they are sharing their experiences, and gaining from each other and from the Bible new light and understanding that enriches their lives. They have the sense of being both teachers and learners and not just passive listeners. The teacher has helped them to learn for themselves, and what they have learned for themselves remains their permanent possession.

4. *Guiding and Controlling the Procedure*

Does this view of teaching lessen the importance of the teacher? By no means! It magnifies and dignifies his office. At no time should the teacher surrender the leadership of the class. His preparation, if wise and thorough, has all been to the end that he may at all times be master of the situation. His control of the procedure will not be arbitrary, but it will be firm and real.

First, *the teacher should control the direction in which thought and discussion move.* He has determined in advance the starting point, and he has clearly in mind the terminus. It is his business to see that the train of ideas does not get stalled, nor go off into side-tracks. A simple outline between the leaves of his Bibles, with the main points on a blackboard in sight of the class, will aid in keeping thought moving in the right direction.

Second, *the teacher will guard carefully the time.* If there are four major points in the lesson, and five minutes are required for getting started and five minutes for summarizing conclusions, it follows that only five minutes can be given to each of the four principle points of the lesson. The lecturer has the advantage of being able to control the time more easily, but the teacher who guides a responsive class may maintain almost as effective control. It must be understood in advance that lengthy speeches and debate are ruled out. The teacher should have this understanding with the class, and privately enlist the co-operation of class officers and key members to shut off the talkative brother or sister who tries to monopolize the discussion. With entire good humor the teacher must learn to interrupt what promises to be a lengthy statement by asking a question, or appealing to the class as a whole. The tactful teacher can soon establish the tradition that nobody except himself talks for more than a minute or two.

Third, *it is the teacher's duty and privilege to draw out the timid members of the class.* Sometimes they can be asked in advance to bring in a bit of information, or answer a question, or express an opinion. The teacher's intimate knowledge of the class will enable him to direct certain questions at members who are especially qualified to give a helpful answer. Often, as the teacher watches the faces before him, he will see some one brighten as an idea or experience comes to mind. This is the signal to the teacher to give the one who is responding silently opportunity for vocal expression.

Fourth, *the teacher can both control and guide the lesson procedure by constant and skillful use of open Bibles* in the hands of members of the class. Is information needed? Is a guiding principle desired? Is a doubtful meaning to be cleared up? Is there difference of opinion? Is light needed on a duty or a doctrine? Let the Bible answer for itself! What more fascinating exercise could be given to men's minds, and what richer food could be provided for their souls, than to have them thus, under wise and skillful guidance, to "search the Scriptures."

A great burden would be rolled from the shoulders of a multitude of teachers of adult Sunday school classes if they could be made to see that they are no longer under the necessity of getting up and getting off speeches before their classes in the name of teaching. There are those who can teach by the lecture method, but they possess training and skill far beyond that of the great masses of teachers. For most of us there is a better way, and this better way is through the conception of teaching as guidance in creative thinking rather than the transmission of ideas.

5. *Arriving at Conclusions*

The Bible is an intensely practical book. It is given to show us how to be saved, how to live the Christian life, how to be happy and useful, how to build better homes, a better society, a better world, and, at length, how to die triumphantly. No lesson has been completely taught that does not arrive at sound and practical conclusions based on the Bible. Not to reach valid and satisfying conclusions is very much like driving a nail and not clinching it, or failing to tie a knot at the end of the thread.

Let us go back to our lesson from the introduction to John's Gospel. The class has spent some twenty-five minutes of intensely interesting thought and discussion growing out of this marvelous passage. They have found out what John meant by calling Jesus Christ the Word; they have examined the thought of the writer as he brings the pre-existent Christ onto the scene of human history. They have sat in awe as the truth has been borne in upon them afresh that the Jesus of history is God, through whom the world was made; they have pondered the words of the Gospel writer as he declares that to as many as received him he gave power to become children of God by a divine rebirth; they have sought to discover the meaning of the witness of John the Baptist when he declared that no man has ever seen God, but that the only begotten Son, who is in the bosom of the Father, has revealed him. The teacher may have guided thought and discussion by means of some such simple outline as this:

(1) Christ the Pre-existent Word;
(2) Christ the Incarnate Word;
(3) Christ the Regenerating Word;
(4) Christ the Revealing Word.

But shall we leave it as a beautiful picture in a frame, at which we have looked and then gone off and left it? If the lesson ends thus, neither mind nor heart will be satisfied. We cry out for dependable, satisfying conclusions. What, now, shall we confidently believe?

(1) That Jesus Christ of the New Testament existed from all eternity, in every respect equal with God the Father;

(2) That he became flesh and dwelt among men, the record of his life being given in the Gospels;

(3) That only through his power, received by faith, can lost men be saved;

(4) That in him we find all we need of God.

The teacher may state these conclusions and beg the class to accept them. A far better way is to lead the class to their discovery, out of the study of the passage itself, and then to get them re-stated in the language of the class members themselves. A blackboard, on which the teacher writes out each conclusion as it is arrived at, will aid in fixing the statements permanently in memory. If all then reverently read in concert what all have shared in formulating, exercise and satisfaction will stamp in the learning so that it will become a very part of each one's mental and spiritual possessions.

6. *Putting Truth into Action*

One thing remains. *What has been learned must be put into practice.* It is not enough to know the truth—we must live the truth. It is doubtful if what we learn from the Scriptures is of much value unless it changes conduct. Indeed, can anything be said truly to have been learned if it makes no difference in behaviour? Christianity is a religion of action, not just a contemplation. Over and over Jesus stressed the necessity of relating truth to duty, doctrine to deeds, light to life. The greatest weakness of all our teaching lies in our failure to induce practical expression of that which we have taught.

On every hand there is crying need for Christianity in action. There are the millions of lost souls, at home and abroad, to be won to Christ; there are other millions to be trained for effective Christian service; there are the sick and needy and overborne, to be cared for and comforted; there are multiplied forms of human activity which need to be transformed by the spirit of Christ; there are vast evils which ought to be uprooted and overthrown in the name and by the power of Christ and his churches; there are warped and twisted personalities that can be made normal and strong only by the love of Christ expressed through human agency. What though Christ be very God, that he came to be our divine-human Saviour, that he can and will save all who come to God through him, that he is the perfect revelation of the Father and the answer to every human need, if millions do not know that this is true and we who do know it are doing little or nothing to make it known to the lost multitudes? The adult Sunday school class should be a mighty force organized for the supreme tasks of soulwinning, teaching and training, comforting and serving.

Christianity must result in better life
God's word believed means action.

Thus alone shall we realize the answer to the prayer which our Lord taught us to pray: "Our Father, who art in heaven, hallowed be thy name, thy kingdom come, thy will be done, as in heaven so on earth."

We have entitled this chapter, "The Teacher in Action." In action an hour on Sunday morning, and inactive the remainder of the week? Not if you are a disciple of the Master Teacher, who went about doing good. The teacher who would be worthy of his high calling must be active in promoting class and departmental organization; active in the business and social meetings of the class; active in visiting absentees and sick members; active in reaching and enrolling new members; active in sympathy and helpfulness toward those in trouble; active in winning the lost; active in co-operation with department and general superintendents and with the pastor and deacons; active as a steward of his time and substance; active in missionary interest and zeal; active in championship of civic and social righteousness. Does this set the standard too high? Would any lower ideal satisfy the Great Teacher, whose we are and whom we serve? Let us dedicate ourselves afresh to the high service to which he has called us as we hear him say: "Ye did not choose me, but I chose you, and appoint you, that ye should go and bear fruit, and that your fruit should abide; that whatsoever ye shall ask of the Father in my name, he may give it you."

AIDS TO LEARNING

1. Look back over the last three or four meetings of your class. How much do you remember of what was taught? Are subjects, main ideas, and conclusions clear and distinct? If not, what do you think interfered with the efficiency of teaching and learning?

2. What plan is followed, in the Adult department or in the general opening assembly, to bring the Bible lesson to the focus of consciousness? Why is it difficult to accomplish this purpose with an assembly program for all ages? If you do not have an Adult department opening program, why not?

3. What is the difference between attention and interest? Why do members of the class often "lose interest"? Suggest several ways in which interest may be sustained.

4. What are some of the dangers of asking questions and otherwise provoking class discussion? Suggest four practical ways in which the teacher may guide and control the procedure. What are the advantages of this kind of teaching over the talk or lecture?

5. Why is it not enough to reach and state the conclusion in words? What is the purpose of learning anything worthwhile? Indicate some present-day needs for the translation of truth into action.

6. Make a list of some forms of activity other than classroom teaching that are demanded of the teacher who measures up to his opportunity and duty and to the example of the Great Teacher.

The principle of tests & measurements can be applied to our teaching — for correct & meaningful teaching will produce outward evidences of inward growth.

CHAPTER IX

TESTING THE RESULTS OF TEACHING

6 tests

OUTLINE

1. The Attendance Test
2. The Knowledge Test
3. The Attitudes Test
4. The Abilities Test
5. The Character Test
6. The Stewardship Test

Many of the most important improvements in education within our lifetime have come about through the application of the principle of tests and measurements. Is a given method sound? Try it out and measure the results: if the results are not satisfactory, in the light of accepted standards, change the method, re-test the changed procedure, and measure the procedure again! Thus, step by step, improvements are made that move in the direction of greater efficiency. The same process applies, as we well know, to all the major field of modern endeavor—agriculture, manufacture, transportation, communication, business, the professions.

Can this principle of tests and measurements be applied in the field of religion? Are not religious values intangible and therefore not measurable? We must admit that there are no scales with which we can measure accurately soul-growth; yet there are outward evidences that change and development are taking place in the spiritual life, and these outward indications can be measured. The tests may not always be valid nor the measurements accurate, but they can be made of great value as a working basis for improvement. Here are six practical tests of the success of your leadership as the teacher of an adult class, by means of which you can at least estimate results, and on the basis of which you can constantly seek improvement in your techniques as teacher, and in the work of the class:

1. *The Attendance Test*

There is a business motto, which reads: "Business goes where it is invited, and stays where it is well-treated." Does not this apply with unusual force to a Sunday school class? In every community there are numbers of adults who do not attend Sunday school for one or both of two reasons: they have never been attractively invited, or, when they did attend they did not get enough out of it to make them want to go back. We no longer measure the greatness of an adult class by its numbers. In fact, we have discovered that when a class goes beyond fifty, it does so at the expense of efficiency in teaching and learning. Our plea is not for big classes that in reality constitute congregations, but for many thoroughly efficient smaller classes with a genuinely educational program. Such classes ought to reach and enlist at least 75 per cent of the church's present and prospective adult constituency.

There is something obviously wrong when a church with, say, three hundred adults in its resident membership and some two hundred on the outside, has fewer than two hundred enrolled in its adult Sunday school classes. The weakness grows more glaring when, with an enrolment of some two hundred, there is an average attendance of about one hundred. Secure the membership roll of your church and count the number of resident adult members. Then take a census of the church community, and discover how many adults, with Baptist preference or no preference, are not attending any Sunday school. Put these two lists together and compare the total with the present adult enrolment in your Sunday school. What percentage of adults is unreached? Now study the average attendance of those enrolled.

What is the percentage of absentees over a period of three months?

Total responsibility cannot be placed upon the teacher, of course, for these unreached multitudes, and for the irregular attendance of members. But if attendance constitutes only a fraction of possibilities, and if absent members are about equal to those present Sunday by Sunday, the teacher ought to go into executive session with himself to determine to what extent he is to blame. It cannot be the Bible's fault that so many are neglecting its study; nor is it entirely the fault of men and women that they are leaving the Bible out of their lives. Perhaps the Bible is not really being taught, and those who attend are not much better off than those who stay away! This is putting it sharply, but maybe we who "teach" carelessly and poorly need to be shocked into a sense of our failure. Intense dissatisfaction with himself is often the first step toward the making of a better teacher.

The teaching for which this book pleads will engender a contagious enthusiasm that will send out those who have enjoyed its privileges and blessings to seek and find others, whom they will bring with them to share its benefits. Adults usually do pretty much what they *want* to do. The sort of teaching described, in a fellowship where every member takes part, and is both giving and receiving a blessing, will make its members *want* to be present more than to stay away. In a very real sense such outcomes are visible tests of the result of teaching. Measured thus, how do you rate?

2. *The Knowledge Test*

The correlative of teaching is learning. If there is no learning there has been no teaching. Learning consists of more than the acquisition of knowledge, but it would be hard to imagine something being learned without an increase of knowledge. The Bible is a book based on facts, events, experiences of actual men and women, exact statements of truth, interpretation of life principles, revelations of spiritual reality. Salvation does not come through knowledge; but knowledge is necessary at every step of the Christian life. Can one repent who does not know what the Bible teaches as to the nature and consequences of sin? Can one exercise saving faith in Jesus Christ who knows nothing about him and his claims as given in the Bible? Can one make an intelligent confession of his faith who does not know what the Bible teaches him to believe? Can one be obedient to the commands of Christ if he does not know what those commands are? Knowledge may be very imperfect, but the Christian life is impossible without a certain amount of knowledge, and this knowledge can be had only through God's Word. True, it may come indirectly, but its original source must be the Bible.

The testing question for the teacher is, How much have the members of my class learned from the Bible that they did not know before I began teaching them? Do they know what the Bible teaches about itself and its authority? Do they know what the Bible teaches about God, his nature, and his purposes? Do they know what the Bible teaches about man, his lost condition and need? Do they know what the Bible teaches about Christ, his life, death, resurrection, and living presence? Do they know what the Bible teaches about the Holy Spirit, his reality, his office, work, his power? Do they know what the Bible teaches about the way to live, joyfully and fruitfully? Do they know what the Bible teaches about immortality, its inexpressible joy for the Christian, and its indescribable suffering for the lost sinner? Do they know the plan of salvation so well that they can lead a lost soul to the Saviour?

Back of such fundamental matters of knowledge lie masses of details out of which these great truths grow. These detailed facts of history, of the lives of men, of the teachings of the prophets, of the deeds and sayings of our Lord, of the acts of the apostles, of the interpretations of Paul and others, of the revelation of John, are valuable not chiefly as interesting information, but as the source from which the great spiritual truths of our religion flow. They are like the fixtures and fittings of a well without which its life-giving water would not be available. If the members of your class do not know these essential facts they are both intellectually and spiritually impoverished.

At regular intervals the teacher should test the knowledge of his class. Old-fashioned, formal written examinations are impracticable, and are considered of doubtful value in modern school practice. There are forms of Bible knowledge tests, however, which are a delight to those who take them. Based on a given number of lessons studied the teacher may devise a certain number of statements that are true, and a certain number that are false. A test of the student's knowledge is the number of these statements that he marks correctly. Again, two or more statements may be combined, only one of which is correct. The student's accurate selection of the best statement in each case is a test of his knowledge. An interesting exercise is to place words or phrases on one side of a column, to be matched by words or phrases on the other side of the column, as, for instance, the names of certain Bible characters, and incidents connected with their lives. The student's knowledge is tested by his ability to match the items correctly. Again, statements may be made, or Scripture passages quoted with key words missing. The test is to fill in correctly the blank spaces. Tests like these, made very brief, may be given in a few minutes, and will form one of the most interesting features of the class program. Carbon or mimeographed copies can be easily provided. Try out this plan of testing the results of your teaching, and on the basis of the result make improvements that will eventually give you a class of real Bible scholars.

3. *The Attitudes Test*

Our lives are largely controlled by our dominant attitudes. An attitude is the direction in which an individual faces, with a tendency to move in that direction. One's attitude toward the church, for instance, may be that of antagonism and indifference, and of course his life moves in the direction of non-attendance and non-support. One may have an attitude of reverence toward the Bible and the things of religion, in which case it is easier for him to attend Sunday school and take part in religious activities. Attitudes are influenced by many things—childhood training, the example of others, fortunate and unfortunate experiences, likes and dislikes, knowledge and ignorance, conscious and unconscious influence. Fortunately attitudes are subject to change and are constantly undergoing change. One of the critical tests of teaching is the extent to which it makes wholesome and desirable changes in attitudes.

What attitudes do members of your class bring with them as they enter the room? It would be exceedingly interesting and valuable if the teacher, through his studies of each member, could answer such questions as these: What is this person's attitude toward God? toward Jesus Christ? toward the Holy Spirit? toward the Bible? toward the church? toward his family? toward his neighbors? toward his work? toward Christian standards of conduct? toward the less fortunate? toward the people of other races? toward the missionary enterprise? toward money and property? toward suffering and misfortune? toward death? What a strange mixture of good and bad attitudes most of us carry around with us! Christian conversion, in its broad sense, is a fundamental change of attitude that turns one from sin and self to Christ and others. But the single experience of conversion, which comes with repentance toward God and faith in Jesus Christ, does not complete the transforming work of grace. Day by day wrong attitudes arise, and day by day they must be changed. Is your teaching actually helping people to make more and more of their attitudes dominantly Christian?

How may the teacher know that he is getting results in changed attitudes on the part of his class? In part, by thoughtful observation. Here is a man who came into the class an unbeliever. His attitude toward Jesus

Christ was one of indifference and rejection. Now he has yielded to the claims of the Saviour, confessed him publicly, obeyed him in baptism, and lined up for service in the church. Surely the teacher can have no doubt that his attitudes have changed! Here is a woman, a nominal Christian, who came into the class with no interest whatever in the Bible. Now she reads her Bible faithfully, is an eager and responsive student, and is an enthusiastic worker in bringing others to the class. No need to ask if her attitudes have changed! Here is a man who enters the class a weak and tempted Christian. He has allowed evil habits to master him and seems almost helpless to escape their power. But the truth brought to him by the teacher, and the warm fellowship of the class, have made available for him the power of the Holy Spirit, and he has become a sober, earnest, dependable Christian. Any one can see that his attitudes have changed. Here is a woman, who before the class claimed her, was nervous, irritable, dissatisfied, worried, a joyless and defeated Christian. But the Word of God, as brought to her by the teacher, and re-enforced by the fellowship of the class, has dwelt richly in her heart, and she has become a serene, happy, useful woman. Of course her attitudes have changed! From time to time the teacher should pass in review each member of the class, seeking to note the changes in attitude which have occurred, and observing those which yet need to be made.

A more direct, and definite test of attitudes may be made in connection with the study of a given series of lessons. At intervals the teacher may pass out sheets of paper on which are certain questions concerning attitudes that may appropriately be raised. Suppose the studies have been in Acts. Such questions as these may be asked: As the result of our studies of the beginnings of Christianity as recorded in the Acts of the Apostles, has the living Christ become more real to you? Are you more deeply assured of his power to save? Have you come to rely more fully on the Holy Spirit? Are you more willing to sacrifice for the cause of Christ as did the early Christians? Are you determined to be a better witness for Christ, seeking to win others to him? Have you attained any higher standards of Christian living? Would you be willing to lay down your life for Christ's sake, as did Stephen? If the Holy Spirit should lay it on your heart, would you be willing to be a missionary to the heathen, as was Paul? If those to whom you tried to take the gospel were to persecute and try to kill you, would you go on witnessing? If you wanted to go in one direction, and the Holy Spirit directed you to go in another, would you gladly yield to the divine will? Have you enough love of Christ in your heart to make you want to take the gospel to Negroes, Italians, Chinese, and others of an alien race? If you were put in jail for being a Christian, would you go on teaching and testifying in the prison? If a man beat you until your back bled, would you turn around and immediately try to win him to Christ? Since the Jews have rejected Christ, do you think you should pray for them and try to win them? If you had to go as a prisoner to testify for Christ, or not go at all, would you stay at home? Do you believe that Christ can and will save all men everywhere who believe? Are you willing to give of your time and strength and money to make Christ known around the world? Do you feel that you are a happier, braver, more useful Christian because of these studies? Every question, it will be observed, can be answered yes or no, or doubtful. A study of these answers will reveal many things to the teacher. The changes in attitudes that have obviously taken place will be a revealing test of the results of his teaching.

4. *The Abilities Test*

Learning worthy of the name should manifest itself in new and enlarged abilities. Modern educational science takes the position that the teacher's first task is "to discover the activities which ought to make up the lives of men and women, and along with these, the abilities and personal qualities necessary for proper performance." The philosophy underlying this conception of education is simply that "education is to help people to do better what they must do anyhow." The teacher of a class of Sunday school adults has a highly specialized job. It is not his business to teach many subjects, but one—religion. His great objective is to help people to live religiously. To do this they need many specific skills, and a reasonable test of the success of his teaching is the extent to which these skills have been acquired. On the basis of observation and occasional written reports the teacher should endeavor to measure the success of his teaching along at least the following four lines:

(1) *Skill in the use and study of the Bible.* Sunday school adults should be familiar with the Bible. They should be able to turn unhesitatingly to any chapter of any book and find an indicated verse. They should know the books of the Bible in their logical groupings— law, history, poetry, major prophets, minor prophets; Gospels, Christian history, letters of Paul, general letters, Revelation. They should have a working vocabulary of Biblical terms, and know the names of the principal characters of the Old and New Testaments. They should be able to trace with reasonable accuracy the course of the history of Israel, the main events in the life of Christ, the travels and missionary labors of Paul and the other apostles. They should be able to use the cross references in the Bible for finding parallel passages, and know how to use a concordance and Bible dictionary.

These abilities should be constantly put to use in actual Bible study. Sunday school adults should know how to study a lesson, how to look up what is unfamiliar, how to discriminate between the more and the less essential, how to use lesson helps, how to organize and outline the results of study, how to report on the work thus done, and how to put what has been learned into practice. If required to give an account of their abilities in the use and study of the Bible, how would the mem-

bers of your class rate? What would this indicate as to
your success or failure as a teacher?

(2) *Skill in expression*. Adults who have attended
Sunday school for years ought to be able to give expression to their ideas with clearness and confidence. They
should have learned to ask and answer questions. They
should have the ability to join intelligently and skilfully in public discussion. They should be able to bear
testimony to their faith, and to share with others their
religious experiences. They should have a sufficient command of the Scriptures to be able to quote its language
in support of their views. Is it not a pity for Christians
to be afflicted with spiritual dumbness after years of
Sunday school attendance? Teaching that has failed to
develop in men and women the ability to express themselves in matters of religion has failed to meet one of
its important tests.

(3) *Skill in church work*. An adult Sunday school
class is not something apart from the church, but is a
part of the church. It is the church at work teaching,
and what is taught should be reflected in efficient church
membership. Sunday school adults who have had the
benefit of years of teaching and training should be competent church workers. Deacons and church officers should
be more efficient in the discharge of their duties. Leaders
in the Training Union and in the Woman's Missionary
Union should fill their offices more capably. Officers of
the class and of the department should learn to function
with increasing ability and satisfaction. Every member
should develop skill in visiting, in building Sunday school
attendance, in welcoming strangers, in making friends
and in being a friend, and in winning others to know and
to love their great Friend. Good teaching should develop
the ability in Christian adults to pray in public, to engage heartily in public worship, and to give wisely and
generously. Let the teacher study his members, and then
standing in the door of his classroom, face out to the
church with the question: To what extent is my teach-

ing producing competent, consecrated, intelligent, devoted church workers? The answer to this question will be a real measure to the success of your teaching.

(4) *Skill in Christian living.* After all, the finest of all arts is the art of Christian living. From their study of the Bible and their experiences in Christian service men and women should learn to live according to the Christian way of life. The most scathing words that Jesus ever uttered were directed against people who knew what the Bible taught but whose living contradicted their profession. He called such people by the harsh name, *hypocrites.* The saddest thing about the hypocritical Pharisees was that they did not recognize themselves as such. Is it not possible for men and women today to study the Bible, to attend Sunday school regularly, and to perform many of the outward functions of religion, yet dissociate all this from their everyday lives?

A question which should be constantly in the mind of the Sunday school teacher is: Are the members of my class living what they are learning? That is, do they practice the teachings of Christ in the home, as neighbors, in business, in politics, at work, at play, in all life's common relationships? If they call Jesus Lord, yet do not the things that he says, he himself declares that he will not recognize them. It is a terribly serious matter for people to learn the theory of Christian living, yet never learn its practice. Measured by this test, how effective is your teaching?

5. *The Character Test*

Back of all conduct is character. Character is what an individual actually is, in the sum total of his knowledge, attitudes, abilities, habits, conduct, and choices. Character may be good or bad. The same qualities of intelligence, industry, energy, purpose, alertness, efficiency, attractiveness might go into the making of a minister or a gangster. The difference would be at the point of *character*—the controlling, unifying purpose of one's life. We speak inaccurately when we say that a person "lacks character." Every one has character, or more accurately is a character. A man may lack good character, and so be a bad character. We are beginning to learn that education, and all the power that goes with knowledge, may be used by men and women of bad character for low and destructive ends. Is not the greatest need of the world today men and women of Christian character?

Teaching that is life-centered should result in learners who are Christ-centered. Paul could say, "for to me to live is Christ." Christ was at the heart of his life, and all else was positionized accordingly. When this may be said of any individual, his character is truly Christian. It is a lifelong task, however, to place and keep everything else in its right relation to Christ as the center. Character is tested daily in scores of ways. Take the names on your class roll and go over them one by one. Ask concerning each member: Does he do right because he is watched? Will he take unfair advantage if undetected? Does he shirk duty when unnoticed? Is he dishonest under pressure of temptation? Does he take pleasure in repeating evil of another? Is he careless and unpunctual in his obligations? Is he harsh and discourteous toward those under his authority? Is he stingy and little in money matters? Is he impure in thought and language? Is he careless of the truth? Is he double-minded and deceitful? Is he cold and unsympathetic toward the needy? Does he blame others for his misfortunes? Does he put his own interests ahead of others? Will he break the law and cause trouble for gain? Is he under the control of an undisciplined temper? If the answer to the majority of these questions is "yes," then you have a man of bad character.

Thank God, the gospel of Jesus Christ can change a man of bad character into a man of good character! Christ can become master, and one by one change these bad traits of character into graces and virtues. This he does, not by magic, but by the power of his Word mediated through Christian influence. The teacher may make a list of these undesirable elements of character, and then with the help of the pastor and two or three trusted officers of the class, may check the members to discover the points at which they are weakest. Thus he may direct his teaching and the influence of the class to the changing of weakness into strength, of selfishness into Christ-likeness. What more glorious success may be asked than the achievement of such results?

6. *The Stewardship Test*

The crowning test of Bible teaching and learning is a life of Christian stewardship. "Ye are not your own," Paul declared, "ye are bought with a price." Christian stewardship is the recognition of God's ownership of oneself and one's possessions, and the joyous committal of all of life to the will of God for the purposes of Jesus Christ under the guidance of the Holy Spirit. To attain this ideal is to reach the highest level of Christian living. The teacher himself will scarcely dare to claim that he had thus attained, but he can say with Paul, "But one thing I do, forgetting the things which are behind, and stretching forward to the things which are before, I press on toward the goal unto the prize of the high calling of God in Christ Jesus." In this holy aspiration, the teacher may test himself and his teaching by four main ways in which Christian stewardship should express itself:

(1) *The stewardship of time.* Our time is not our own. How are we using it? What proportion of it is wasted? How much of it is spent selfishly? How much time do we give to God in prayer, meditation, worship, Bible study? How much is spent in the unselfish service of others? Raise these questions with your class, and measure your teaching by their answers.

(2) *The stewardship of talents.* Our talents are not our own. Every ability that we have is a gift of God, and God has the right to claim its use in his service. As you think of yourself and the members of your class, you may well ask: What talents are here represented? to

what extent are they being developed? in what ways are they being utilized in the service of Christ and others? How much talent is going to waste? How may the special ability of each member be harnessed to the work of the class? to the work of the church and of the Kingdom? What measure of success of your teaching is thus revealed?

(3) *The stewardship of influence.* Influence is the impact of one life upon another. Our influence is not our own. It is the gift of God for the shaping of other lives. Contemplating the class the questions arise: Is our influence for good or evil? Are we a stumbling block to others? Are lives made poorer or richer because of contacts with us? Is our influence confined to a narrow circle, or does it reach to the ends of the earth? What may we do to make our influence count for more? Tested by these questions, what is the measure of your success as a teacher?

(4) *The stewardship of possessions.* Our property is not our own. "The silver and the gold," God says, "are mine." Tithing is one of the best expressions of property stewardship. How many tithers are there in the class? How many give systematically and proportionately to the church? How many act as if their money were their own, to do with as they please? How many are masters of their possessions and how many have been mastered by their possessions? Who seem to have fallen victims to the sin of covetousness? Who have learned the joy of using not one-tenth only but all of their possessions as under the will of God? How does your teaching stand this test?

Jesus said, "By their fruits ye shall know them." This is the ultimate test of what we are, what we do, and what we teach. His teaching stood the test of results in the lives of the men and women whom he gathered about him, and still stands the test wherever mediated through the personality of teachers who have his spirit and are wholly committed to him and his service. God grant that our teaching, too, may stand the test both here and in that day when we shall give account to God of the stewardship of our high calling!

AIDS TO LEARNING

1. Name some of the improvements in the world of science and invention that have come through testing and measuring. Why is it more difficult to apply the principle of tests and measurements to religion?

2. What changes should be made, in your opinion, in the present method of teaching adults in your Sunday school in order to secure the attendance of unreached possibilities? How go about securing these changes?

3. What is an "attitude"? What are some of the most important life attitudes? How are attitudes changed? Indicate how the teacher may check up to discover the extent to which attitudes are being changed or strengthened.

4. From what to what is one converted on becoming a Christian? Why is the character test the supreme test of Bible teaching? What are some life questions that constitute tests of character?

5. Re-state in your own words the doctrine of Christian stewardship. Give four main ways in which stewardship should find expression in the life of a Christian. To what extent are these results manifest in the members of your class? what does this test reveal as to the character and quality of teaching?

6. After all, who is to be the final judge of our success or failure? Which are the better tests—learning and skilfulness, or love and faithfulness? What reward may we expect when we shall have done the best we can with what we have?

DIRECTIONS FOR THE TEACHING AND STUDY OF THIS BOOK FOR CREDIT

I. Directions for the Teacher

1. Ten class periods of forty-five minutes each, or the equivalent, are required for the completion of a book for credit.

2. The teacher should request an award on the book taught.

3. The teacher shall give a written examination covering the subject matter in the textbook. The examination may take the form of assigned work to be done between the class sessions, in the class sessions, or as a final examination.

Exception: All who attend all of the class sessions; who read the book through by the close of the course; and who, in the judgment of the teacher, do the classwork satisfactorily may be exempted from taking the examination.

4. Application for Sunday school awards should be sent to the state Sunday school department on proper application forms. These forms should be made in triplicate. Keep the last copy for the church file, and send the other two copies.

II. Directions for the Student*

(*The student must be fifteen years of age or older to receive Sunday school credit.)

1. In Classwork

(1) The student must attend at least six of the ten forty-five minute class periods to be entitled to take the class examination.

(2) The student must certify that the textbook has been read. (In rare cases where students may find it impracticable to read the book before the completion of the classwork, the teacher may accept a promise to read the book carefully within the next two weeks. This applies only to students who do the written work.)

(3) The student must take a written examination, making a minimum grade of 70 per cent, or qualify according to *Exception* noted above.

2. In Individual Study by Correspondence

Those who for any reason wish to study the book without the guidance of a teacher will use one of the following methods:

(1) Write answers to the questions printed in the book, or

(2) Write a summary of each chapter or a development of the chapter outlines.

In either case the student must read the book through.

Students may find profit in studying the text together, but where awards are requested, individual papers are required. Carbon copies or duplicates in any form cannot be accepted.

All written work done by such students on books for Sunday school credit should be sent to the state Sunday school secretary.

III. This Book Gives Credit in Section V of the Sunday School Training Course.